The Unwritten Rules Are Meant to be Broken

The Unwritten Rules Are Meant to be Broken

Breaking Barriers, Thriving in Corporate Spaces, and Redefining Success as a Black Leader

Sharitta Marshall

Edited by Ashara Hood

Intentional Living Publications

The Unwritten Rules Are Meant to be Broken Copyright © 2025 by Intentional Living Publications

All rights reserved.

No part of this publication may be reproduced, stored, or transmitted in any form or by any means, electronic, mechanical, photocopying, recording, scanning, or otherwise, except as permitted under Section 107 or 108 of the 1976 United States Copyright Act, without the prior written permission of the author.

Requests to the author and publisher for permission should be addressed to the following email: info@visionarydevelopmentinc.com

Limitation of liability/disclaimer of warranty: This publication is designed to provide accurate and authoritative information regarding the subject matter covered. It is sold with the understanding that the publisher is not engaged in rendering legal or other professional services. If you require legal advice of other expert assistance, you should seek the services of an appropriate professional.

While the author has made every effort to provide accurate internet information at the time of publication, neither the publisher nor the author assumes responsibility for errors or changes that occur after publication. Further, the publisher does not have any control over and does not assume any responsibility for author or third-party websites or their content.

Published in the United States by Intentional Living Publications. A publishing house under Visionary Development Inc.

ISBN: (hardcover) 978-1-7351171-5-7 | ISBN: (paperback) 978-1-7351171-6-4 | ISBN: (eBook) 978-1-7351171-7-1

*For those that weren't seen, heard, and valued.
It's time to take up all the space.*

Contents

Prologue i

Introduction: Why This Book? Why Now? iii

Chapter 1: Owning Your Worth in a System That Doesn't Always See It 1
    Disowning Imposter Syndrome and Owning Your Unique Strengths 1
    Recognizing the Value You Bring 9
    The "Invisible Work" Trap 11
    Conclusion 13

Chapter 2: The Leadership Mindset 15
    Transitioning from Task Execution to Strategic Thinking 15
    Understanding the Difference Between Leading and Managing 23
    Shifting Focus from "Doing the Work" to "Guiding the Work" 29
    Conclusion 39

Chapter 3: Staying Authentic in the Corporate Arena 41
    Strategies to Resist Code-Switching (Hint: It Has Nothing to Do with Professionalism) 42
    Navigating Microaggressions and Addressing Bias with Confidence 48
    The Mental Toll of Microaggressions: Protecting Your Energy 53
    Personal Stories of Black Leaders Who Thrived Authentically 55
    Conclusion 60

Chapter 4: Innovation Through Creativity 63

    Leveraging Your Unique Perspective to Solve Problems in New Ways 63
    Strategies for Leveraging Your Unique Perspective 64
    Why Leveraging Your Perspective Builds Leadership Credibility 67
    Strategies to Present Unconventional Ideas in Traditional Spaces.. 69
    Examples of How Creativity Builds Leadership Credibility.. 75
    The Link Between Creativity and Credibility 78
    Actionable Takeaways for Building Leadership Credibility Through Creativity 78
    Conclusion... 80

Chapter 5: Thinking Big – Critical Thinking and Decision Making 83
    Learning to Make Decisions with Limited Information... 84
    Balancing Risk and Reward in Leadership.. 89
    Exercises: Create Your Own Case Studies for Honing Critical Thinking Skills 91
    Conclusion... 92

Chapter 6: Building Bridges – Collaboration and Influence 93
    The Art of Building Allies Across Departments and Levels... 93
    Tips for Navigating Difficult Team Dynamics While Maintaining Harmony........................ 96
    Exercises to Strengthening Your Collaborative Skills 98
    Conclusion... 102

Chapter 7: Owning the Room – Communication for Impact 103
    Crafting Your Message for Clarity and Persuasion 103
    Public Speaking and Storytelling as Leadership Tools 105
    Handling Tough Conversations with Poise 106

Exercises: Enhancing Your Communication Skills.. 108
Exercise 2: Storytelling for Impact............ 109
Exercise 3: Role-Playing Tough Conversations 110
Conclusion 111

Chapter 8: Setting Your Sights on the C-Suite.... 113
Creating a Vision for Your Career 113
SMART Goal Setting Tailored to Your Professional Journey 115
Exercises: Writing Your Leadership Development Plan 117
Example Leadership Development Plan Structure: 120
Conclusion 122

Chapter 9: Self-Advocacy Without Apology........123
Asking for What You Want—and Getting It 123
How to Highlight Your Achievements While Remaining a Team Player...........................125
Building a Personal Brand That Speaks for Itself 126
Conclusion 128

Chapter 10: Mentorship and Sponsorship 129
The Difference Between Mentors and Sponsors— and Why You Need Both 129
How to Cultivate Relationships That Open Doors 131
Tips for Navigating Cross-Identity Mentorship Dynamics 133
Conclusion 136

Chapter 11: Leading While Black.........................137
Understanding the Unique Burdens and Privileges of Being a Black Leader 137
Strategies for Addressing Bias in Your Team or Organization 140
How to Balance Being a Role Model with Protecting Your Peace.................................. 141

Conclusion 142

Chapter 12: Resilience Without Burnout 143
    Setting Boundaries to Protect Your Time and
    Mental Health 143
    Recognizing and Addressing Burnout Before It
    Derails Your Progress 145
    The Role of Therapy, Self-Care, and Community
    in Long-Term Success 146
    Conclusion 148

Chapter 13: Pay It Forward 149
    Becoming a Mentor/Sponsor and Advocate for
    Others 149
    Building a Legacy of Leadership That Reflects
    Your Values 151
    Contributing to Systemic Change from Within
    152
    Conclusion 153

Conclusion: A Call to Lead 155
    Why Authenticity Matters in an Ecosystem that
    doesn't always see you 155
    Action Plan: Taking the Next Steps in Your
    Leadership Journey 157
    Final Thoughts 159

Prologue

As I write this in early 2025, in the United States we find ourselves in a time of reckoning—a period where conversations around diversity, equity, and inclusion (DEI) have been both amplified and challenged. The path forward feels uncertain, yet one thing is clear: the fight for equitable opportunities and spaces remains as urgent as ever.

Like so many others, who have endured the weight of "corporate PTSD," I write this book as a Black woman who has successfully recovered from corporate PTSD. It's the accumulation of years of navigating systemic barriers, confronting microaggressions and macroaggressions, and managing the unspoken, but ever-present, expectation to overachieve simply to be seen as adequate. I base this book on the things that went wrong, the firings, the layoffs, the underemployment, the bad managers and horrible coworkers, the "woulda, coulda, shoulda," all the things that happened to myself and others that we allowed to derail the career we deserved. However, this book is not a lament. It is a declaration of resilience, a guide for transformation, and a reflection of the strength I've found—not just in my own journey, but in the collective experiences of countless Black professionals across the world.

Within the corporate ecosystem, the challenge for Black leaders is not only to seize opportunities for growth but also to navigate the subtle, often unspoken barriers that persist: microaggressions, implicit biases, and the unwritten rules of corporate culture.

This book, and the development program it represents, is born out of the need to equip Black professionals with the tools to thrive without unnecessary compromise. It is an invitation to embrace the dual responsibility of pursuing individual excellence while driving systemic change. Leadership, after all, is not just a position, it's a commitment to influence, integrity, and impact.

Throughout this journey, you will find insights that speak directly to the realities of being a Black professional in today's corporate spaces. From dismantling imposter syndrome to mastering self-advocacy, from building your personal brand to navigating corporate culture, this book provides actionable strategies rooted in the unique experiences of Black leaders. But more than that, it affirms the truth that you belong in every room you enter, and that your leadership is both necessary and powerful.

Introduction: Why This Book? Why Now?

If you're a Black professional working your way up the corporate ladder, you know that navigating these spaces can be both a formidable challenge and an act of resilience. From the subtle biases to the overt microaggressions, and the lack of representation at higher levels and boards, the journey to leadership is often riddled with obstacles that are unique to our experiences.

For many of us, the corporate world has been designed with a certain profile in mind—a profile that often does not include Black professionals. This reality can manifest in different ways: being overlooked for opportunities, having to prove your competence over and over again, or being asked to represent an entire race instead of just yourself. It's exhausting, and it can make you question whether your ambition, vision, and identity have a place at the table.

Example: Consider the professional who's constantly asked to speak on diversity issues but is overlooked for strategic leadership roles.

The challenges are real. And they're part of a larger systemic inequities that's slow to change. But that doesn't mean you can't find success. It also doesn't mean that you can't reach the heights of leadership you aspire to and do so without sacrificing who you are in the process.

The Dual Burden of Navigating Systemic Barriers While Staying Authentic

One of the most difficult parts of rising to leadership is finding the balance between navigating systemic barriers and staying true to who you are. It's easy to be tempted to conform, to adopt behaviors or mindsets that don't feel natural, just to be seen, heard, and valued or just merely keep your job. But that comes at a cost: your peace, your self-worth, possibly your health (mentally and physically), and ultimately, your effectiveness as a leader.

Reflection Point: *How many times have you second-guessed yourself, or dimmed your light to make others more comfortable?*

What toll has that taken on your sense of identity and purpose?

What toll has it taken on your mental and physical health?

The key to success lies not just in overcoming barriers, but in navigating them in a way that allows you to thrive while staying authentic. This book is your guide to doing exactly that—reaching for the top, or however you define success without sacrificing your values, identity, health or sense of self.

The Purpose of This Book: A Roadmap to Leadership Without Compromise

The intention behind this book is simple: to provide you with the tools, insights, and inspiration to step into your full leadership potential, unapologetically and confidently. This is not a book about climbing the corporate ladder; it's a guide to building a career that aligns with who you are and what you stand for.

Each chapter has been carefully crafted to address the specific challenges you may face and provide you with actionable strategies and reflections. Whether you're looking to dismantle imposter syndrome, shift your mindset to strategic thinking, communicate effectively, or build relationships that support your career, this book is here to guide you.

What You'll Gain:

- **A Strong Sense of Self:** Learn how to recognize your worth and leverage your strengths without changing who you are.
- **Leadership Strategies:** Gain insight into building teams, navigating difficult conversations, and presenting your ideas persuasively.
- **Resilience Without Burnout:** Discover how to set boundaries and take care of your mental health as you pursue leadership goals.
- **Mentorship and Sponsorship Guidance:** Learn how to cultivate relationships that propel your career forward and contribute to your legacy.

A Message of Empowerment: "You Don't Have to Fit In to Rise Up."

This is a reminder and a challenge. You don't have to contort yourself, diminish your voice, or hide parts of your identity to move forward; that's not to say that what you are doing may have been a form of protection, mentally or physically. What I am saying is that your leadership journey is not about fitting into a mold; it's about ignoring the mold and creating spaces where others can follow.

Example: Picture a leader who achieves a C-suite position and, instead of conforming to the status quo, brings their full, authentic self to work—sharing their culture, their perspective, and their values. This leader becomes a model for others, showing that success doesn't mean erasing who you are but amplifying it. Now imagine that this leader is you.

The path ahead may be difficult, and the road may be longer than it is for others, but it is yours to travel with pride and purpose. This book is here to equip you with the knowledge, strategies, and confidence to lead on your own terms.

Your leadership matters, and you deserve to thrive as your true self. It's time to move from surviving in corporate spaces to thriving—and to inspire others to do the same.

Skills for the Journey – Mastering Core Competencies

Every successful journey requires a set of tools, and the path to leadership is no different. Especially when navigating corporate spaces, mastering core competencies isn't just about meeting expectations, it's about standing out, overcoming challenges, and transforming obstacles into opportunities.

The chapters in this section are designed to equip you with the essential skills that every leader needs to thrive. But these aren't just technical skills, they're the tools that allow you to lead authentically, build influence, and create meaningful impact in spaces that weren't always designed with you in mind.

Chapter 4: Innovation Through Creativity focuses on the power of your unique perspective. As a Black professional, you bring experiences and insights that others may overlook, and these differences are the foundation of creative problem-solving. You'll learn how to present unconventional ideas in traditional spaces and see how creativity can elevate your leadership credibility.

Chapter 5: Thinking Big – Critical Thinking and Decision-Making helps you sharpen your ability to evaluate complex situations and make sound decisions, even with limited information. Balancing risk and reward is part of every leadership role, and this chapter will give you the tools to approach challenges with confidence and precision.

Chapter 6: Building Bridges – Collaboration and Influence dives into the art of connecting with others. Leadership isn't about working alone—it's about building relationships that span departments, personalities, and perspectives. You'll explore strategies to foster collaboration, lead diverse teams, and manage conflict with grace and effectiveness.

Chapter 7: Owning the Room – Communication for Impact focuses on one of the most critical leadership skills: the ability to communicate with clarity and confidence. Whether you're giving a presentation, sharing your story, or navigating a tough conversation, your voice matters. This chapter will help you hone your communication skills to inspire, influence, and lead with impact.

Why These Skills Matter

These skills aren't just "nice to have"—they are the foundation of effective leadership. They allow you to:

- Solve problems creatively and position yourself as a thought leader.
- Make decisions that drive results and navigate uncertainty with confidence.
- Build relationships that amplify your influence and foster a culture of collaboration.

- Communicate your vision and values with authenticity and impact.

Mastering these competencies is about more than professional success. It's about showing that leadership doesn't require you to conform—it requires you to be bold, authentic, and unapologetically you.

As you move through this section, think of these chapters as your toolkit. Each skill is a steppingstone to navigating the challenges ahead, breaking down barriers, and building a career that reflects your values, ambitions, and unique strengths.

Let's dive in and start mastering the skills that will define your leadership journey.

Chapter 1: Owning Your Worth in a System That Doesn't Always See It

Disowning Imposter Syndrome and Owning Your Unique Strengths

The concept of "Imposter Syndrome" describes a psychological pattern where individuals doubt their accomplishments and fear being exposed as a "fraud or diversity hire". While this framing for us suggests only an internal flaw, it fails to address the societal and structural biases that contribute to these feelings, particularly for Black professionals and other underrepresented groups.

Historically, the dominant narratives of success have centered on whiteness as the default standard. This cultural bias marginalizes the contributions and achievements of non-white individuals, creating environments where systemic inequities are internalized as personal inadequacies. By disowning the fallacy of imposter syndrome, we can reject these biased narratives and reclaim the truth: the problem lies in exclusionary systems, not in our abilities.

1. The Origins and Biases Behind the Fallacy

The term "Imposter Syndrome" was coined in the 1970s by psychologists Dr. Pauline Clance and Dr. Suzanne Imes. While their research illuminated patterns of self-doubt, it failed to contextualize how systemic inequities perpetuate these feelings.

Some Key Drivers:

- **Cultural Biases:** Corporate environments often treat "whiteness and maleness" as the standard for competence, marginalizing others by default.
- **Stereotypes:** Black professionals are often labeled as "diversity hires" or presumed less qualified, regardless of their actual credentials.
- **Underrepresentation:** A lack of diverse leadership reinforces feelings of not belonging, shifting the blame onto individuals rather than systemic issues.

2. The Real Impact of Systemic Bias

Career Barriers:

- **Limited Opportunities:** Biases often gatekeep access to leadership roles, leaving qualified professionals overlooked.
- **Overcompensation:** Marginalized individuals often overwork to counteract perceptions of inadequacy, leading to burnout.
- **Invisible Labor:** Many Black professionals carry the additional burden of advocating for diversity while performing their job roles. This can also lead to them being labeled as aggressive or arrogant.

Mental Health Consequences:

- **Internalized Oppression:** Repeated exposure to microaggressions and exclusion fosters self-

doubt.
- **Chronic Stress:** Constantly navigating systemic bias leads to exhaustion, diminished well-being, and other physical ailments.
- **Heightened Anxiety:** The pressure to constantly prove oneself, avoid negative stereotypes, and navigate workplace bias can lead to persistent anxiety, impacting focus, decision-making, and overall job performance.

<u>**Financial Impact:**</u>
- **Wage Disparities:** Black professionals often earn less than their white counterparts for the same work due to systemic pay inequities. This doesn't even begin to address the intersectionality-based disparities for many Black professionals.
- **Limited Access to Promotions:** Fewer promotions mean slower salary growth, reduced earning potential over time, and lower lifetime wealth accumulation.
- **Higher Turnover Costs:** Many Black employees leave organizations due to unaddressed biases, leading to career disruptions, job instability, and lost income during transitions.
- **Wealth Gap Reinforcement:** The compounded effect of wage gaps, slower promotions, and higher turnover contributes to the racial wealth gap, limiting opportunities for generational wealth-building.

My Story

I used to think that if I simply just worked harder, stayed positive, and followed all the rules, my effort would be enough in my position. I surmised that my merit and dedication would speak for itself. But the truth was, corporate America had a different plan for me.

It started subtly. A comment here, a shift in tone there. "Your demeanor carries the entire team, so if you're not smiling and happy, it brings everyone down." I wasn't the manager, yet somehow, I was expected to emotionally regulate an entire team. Even when we transitioned to remote work, I was the unspoken "mood monitor". If I was quiet or simply having a normal, neutral day, I was met with, "Is everything okay? You seem off." There was no room for me to just exist. I had to perform happiness, even at my own expense.

It wasn't long after that came the blatant inequities. A co-worker, who started almost a year after me, was promoted to a management position I had applied for—for the second time. Despite my qualifications, my experience, my education, and my efforts to follow every piece of advice given to position myself for advancement, I was told that he was simply "more experienced." When I asked what I needed to do differently to obtain a promotion, I was met with vague, placating responses. The truth was, I could do everything right and still not be seen as deserving.

When I simply tried to connect with the only other Black person in my department—someone I needed to speak to in order to complete projects—I was threatened with a verbal warning. When I asked how this was negatively impacting my work, I was told, "It's about perception." Not productivity, not performance—just the perception of two Black employees conversing in a shared workspace. Meanwhile, my white colleagues freely congregated, laughed, and chatted for extended periods without reprimand.

The contradictions never ended. During one performance review, I was told that I "smiled too much" and needed to work on it. No further explanation, no constructive feedback. Just another impossible standard to decipher, and yet another way that caused me to question myself.

In a different instance, I was called arrogant and told no one wanted to work with me. When I asked for clarification—for example, for specific feedback, for anything actionable— no one was able to share any valuable feedback with me. I got nothing. It was just another label appended onto my character, and another way that caused me to shrink myself to fit into a space that refused to make room for me.

Each of these experiences, although with different companies and teams, compounded over time, wore me down. The constant gaslighting, the microaggressions that grew into macroaggressions, the expectation to be perfect but never celebrated. It took a toll on my mind, my body, and my spirit. The anxiety became unbearable. I second-guessed everything about myself—the way I spoke, the way I sat, the way I walked into a room. I would stay up late replaying conversations in my head, wondering if I had unknowingly done something "wrong" again. I found myself dreading work, experiencing panic attacks before, during and after work, and feeling utterly exhausted from the sheer effort of existing in a space that barely tolerated me.

Even with therapy, it took years for me to unlearn the idea that if I contorted myself enough, I would finally be accepted. The reality is, no amount of shrinking, smiling, or overachieving can fix an environment that refuses to acknowledge your worth. It took an even longer time to realize that the toll this took on my mental health wasn't just a personal burden, it was a systemic issue, designed to exhaust and erode people like me until we either conformed completely or left altogether.

I share this story not to dishearten you, but to affirm you. If you've ever felt like you were drowning under the weight of these pressures, I need you to know: it's not you. It was never you. You deserve to be seen, heard, and valued for who you are—not just for how well you can endure mistreatment. Because the alternative is not an option.

3. Disowning the Fallacy: Strategies for Liberation

Step 1: Reframe the Narrative

Replace the "fraud" or "diversity hire" narrative with one of empowerment. Recognize that feelings of inadequacy often stem from external, or even internal biases, rather than internal deficiencies.

Step 2: Build Collective Validation

- **Engage in Community:** Join Employee Resource Groups (ERGs) or professional networks that affirm your worth and amplify your voice.
- **Mentorship:** Seek guidance from those who understand and counter systemic barriers.

Step 3: Advocate for Structural Change

- **Challenge Biases:** Push for equitable hiring, promotion practices, and leadership accountability.
- **Normalize Diversity:** Amplify diverse voices and successes to dismantle the myth of a single standard for excellence.

Step 4: Celebrate Your Power

- **Affirm Your Achievements:** Document and reflect on your successes (great and small) as acts of resilience against systemic bias.
- **Set Boundaries:** Reject perfectionism and

prioritize your well-being.
- **Claim Space:** Take pride in your contributions and reject narratives that diminish your worth.

4. Practical Tools and Exercises for Empowerment

Suggested Journaling Prompts:

- Reflect on three significant accomplishments and the steps you took to achieve them.
- Identify recurring thoughts of self-doubt and reframe them with evidence of your success.
- Document instances where systemic bias or microaggressions impacted your confidence and explore actionable responses.

Example Affirmations:

- "My achievements reflect my skills and dedication, not external validation."
- "I reject systems that devalue my worth and embrace my power."
- "I contribute uniquely and meaningfully to every space I occupy."

Visualization Exercises:

- Envision yourself confidently leading a project, team or receiving well-deserved recognition.
- Practice visualizing challenging situations and your empowered responses.

Action Steps:

1. Create a "success portfolio" documenting achievements, feedback, and growth.
2. Engage in self-care routines to prioritize mental and emotional well-being. This includes starting with you at the top of the list.

3. Set short-term goals for self-advocacy in professional spaces.

5. Resources for Empowerment and Advocacy

Books:
- "You Belong: A Call for Connection" by Sebene Selassie.
- "The Memo: What Women of Color Need to Know to Secure a Seat at the Table" by Minda Harts.

Podcasts:
- "Truth's Table" - A podcast on Black women's experiences and empowerment.
- "Dear Black CEO" - Highlighting Black professionals' journeys to success.

TED Talks:
- "The Danger of a Single Story" by Chimamanda Ngozi Adichie — Challenging stereotypes.
- "How to Build Your Confidence - And Spark It in Others" by Brittany Packnett Cunningham.

Tools:
- Join ERGs that center marginalized voices.
- Advocate for diversity metrics and inclusive policies in your workplace.
- Accompanying Professional Guide Journal (available separately from this book)
- Accompanying Professional Guide Planner (available separately from this book)

Disowning the fallacy of imposter syndrome is not merely a personal journey but a collective act of liberation. By rejecting narratives rooted in systemic bias, we affirm our inherent worth and advocate for equitable workplaces. Together, we dismantle the structures that perpetuate self-doubt and reclaim spaces where all talents are recognized and celebrated.

Recognizing the Value You Bring

Every skill, every achievement, and every hard-won lesson has brought you to this moment, and each of those experiences holds value. Yet, many of us downplay our contributions because we've been conditioned to think that excelling is simply "part of the job"—that we shouldn't celebrate solving problems or adding perspective. This habit is often compounded by systems that overlook, undervalue, or even appropriate our work. But here's the truth: **your value is non-negotiable**—and it's time to see it, claim it, and articulate it unapologetically.

Think about some of the challenges that you've overcome:

- *Did you find solutions to persistent problems your team or company couldn't solve?*
- *Did you offer a perspective no one else had, opening new doors to innovation?*
- *Did you bring the team together in the face of conflict, tension, or burnout?*
- *Did you deliver outcomes despite being overlooked, underestimated, or unsupported?*

These aren't "small wins"—they are proof of the value you bring to the table, even if you didn't articulate them at the time.

Stop Seeking External Validation

The system you're navigating may not always acknowledge your contributions, but that doesn't mean they lack value. Waiting for someone else to validate your worth will leave you second-guessing yourself. When you claim your strengths and successes, you shift from **seeking approval** to **commanding respect**.

Reframe Your Mindset: See Yourself as a Brand

Your career is a reflection of your distinct strengths, skills, and experiences. Start viewing yourself as a **brand**—a unique combination of attributes that set you apart from everyone else in the room.

- *What are you known for?* Do you solve complex problems? Bring calm under pressure? Build bridges across teams?
- *What do you bring that no one else does?* Your lived experiences, perspective, and creativity add value that others may not replicate.
- *Where do you thrive?* Identify the environments, projects, or challenges where you shine brightest.

The more clearly you recognize your own value, the less likely you are to shrink, contort, or play small to fit into someone else's box.

The "Invisible Work" Trap

One challenge that many of us often face is carrying the weight of "invisible work" without recognition. You may find yourself:

- Being the default team player, always asked to take on extra tasks without acknowledgement.
- Mediating conflicts or mentoring colleagues—while others receive credit for the "tangible" work.
- Being the mascot, entertainer, or carrier for the others emotional wellbeing or the team's happiness.
- Being tasked with educating others about diversity, equity, and inclusion—on top of your formal responsibilities, without additional compensation or acknowledgment.

Recognizing your value means calling out the work you do, even if it goes unnoticed. Document your impact regularly:

- *What problem did you solve today?*
- *Who benefited from your contributions?*
- *What were the results?*

By quantifying your achievements, you position yourself to advocate for recognition, promotions, and opportunities more effectively.

Exercise: **Identifying Your Strengths and Core Values**

1. **Strength Inventory**:
    - Write down 5-10 accomplishments you're proud of in your career. Be specific about what you did, the skills you used, and the impact you created.

- Ask trusted colleagues, mentors, or friends: "What do you think I do exceptionally well?" Sometimes others see our strengths more clearly than we do.

2. **Core Values Reflection**:
    - What principles guide the way you work? (e.g., integrity, collaboration, innovation, equity)
    - When have you felt most fulfilled or proud in your career? What values were aligned in those moments?
    - Which values feel non-negotiable for you, even in challenging environments?

Putting it Together:

Once you've outlined your strengths and values, write a clear statement that captures the unique value you bring. For example:

"I'm a problem-solver who thrives in challenging environments. I excel at bringing teams together to deliver innovative solutions, and I'm guided by a commitment to equity, collaboration, and driving measurable results."

When you know your worth, you stop shrinking to make others comfortable. Instead, you show up confidently, authentically, and ready to make the impact you were destined for.

Conclusion

Knowing your worth starts with rejecting the lies of imposter syndrome and embracing your unique strengths and values. As you continue through this journey, these truths will become the foundation for your personal brand, career goals, and leadership style. Write down one affirmation you'll commit to every morning—something that reminds you that you're not just capable but extraordinary.

When you're ready, we'll build on this foundation in the next chapter to navigate systems of bias while staying true to yourself.

Chapter 2: The Leadership Mindset

Transitioning from Task Execution to Strategic Thinking

When you've excelled as an individual contributor, your ability to execute tasks efficiently is often celebrated. You're seen as the go-to person for delivering results, meeting deadlines, and keeping projects on track. While these are invaluable skills, they can inadvertently become a trap. This success can lead to being **pigeonholed as "the reliable worker" or "the doer"**, the one who delivers, not the one who decides, innovates, or drives the bigger vision. Meanwhile, others are often seen as the "strategic thinkers" or "visionaries."

Breaking Out of the "Doer" Box

The transition to strategic thinking requires intentional repositioning. It's about shifting the focus from *"What can I get done today?"* to ***"How can I shift the team or organization long-term?"***

Strategic thinking is what separates managers and leaders from task executors. It's about anticipating future challenges, recognizing patterns, and making decisions that align with organizational goals.

Breaking out of the "doer" box is not just a matter of skill; it's about **challenging biases that limit how your potential is perceived**. You're not just a worker—you're a strategist, a visionary, and a problem-solver who can drive business success.

Why This Matters:

Corporate systems often reward task execution because it's tangible and easy to measure. However, strategic thinking is where real leadership begins. Unfortunately, as a Black professional you may encounter systemic biases that confine you to execution roles, sidelining you from opportunities to lead or make high-impact decisions.

To overcome this, you must:

1. **Challenge the Narrative**: Demonstrate that you're not just delivering results but driving outcomes that align with the organization's strategy.
2. **Showcase Your Insights**: Proactively communicate how your work ties to the bigger picture, creating value beyond immediate deliverables.
3. **Advocate for High-Impact Opportunities**: Seek out or suggest projects that require strategic planning and leadership, rather than just tactical execution.

The Stakes Are High: If you don't make this transition intentionally, you risk being seen as indispensable for your *current* role but invisible for higher-level leadership opportunities.

How to Start Thinking Strategically

1. Ask Bigger Questions:

Instead of focusing solely on what needs to be done, you can ask:
- "What problem are we solving, and why does it matter?"
- "What long-term goals does this project/task support?"
- "What opportunities exist to innovate and improve this process?"

Please keep in mind that there may be those that may "feel" as though you are challenging them versus, strategically addressing the matter. You may want to start off with "thinking strategically" or "looking at the bigger picture" to keep the narrative focused on the matter, not a person.

2. **Connect the Dots:** Look for patterns across projects, teams, and departments. Strategic leaders see relationships others miss and use these insights to drive efficiencies and results.

3. **Own the Narrative:** When presenting updates or achievements, don't just talk about tasks completed—highlight outcomes, challenges overcome, and the broader value delivered to the organization.

Example: Instead of saying, *"I delivered the quarterly report ahead of schedule,"* reframe it as:
"I delivered the quarterly report early, which allowed leadership to make informed decisions and course-correct mid-cycle, improving resource allocation by 15%."

Action Step: *Before diving into any task, pause and "ask the bigger" questions. Document your answers so you can refer back to them when presenting outcomes.*

2. Connect the Dots:

Strategic leaders excel at recognizing patterns and relationships that others miss. They see the big picture, link individual projects to overarching business goals, and identify opportunities for efficiency, innovation, and growth.

How to Connect the Dots:

- Look for trends across projects, teams, or processes. Ask: "What common issues or opportunities do I see?"
- Identify dependencies between teams or departments that could be optimized.
- Highlight how your work supports cross-functional success, not just siloed objectives.

Example: As a marketing manager, Maya frequently worked with both the sales and product teams. She noticed a troubling pattern: sales reps were promising features to clients that the product team had not yet built, leading to missed expectations, frustrated customers, and tense internal meetings. At first, Maya found herself caught in the middle, relaying information between the two teams, but she realized that this was a recurring issue, not a one-time miscommunication.

Rather than simply escalating complaints, Maya took a leadership approach. She started by asking key questions: *Why was this happening repeatedly? What underlying gaps were causing the misalignment?* After talking to both teams, she discovered that sales was not aware of the product development roadmap, and the product team wasn't getting real-time customer feedback from sales. The teams operated in silos, and there was no clear process for cross-functional collaboration.

Recognizing the need for a sustainable solution, Maya proposed and facilitated a monthly *Sales-Product Alignment Meeting*. This forum allowed sales to share client demands early, while the product team provided updates on upcoming features. Over time, this reduced friction, improved planning, and enabled the company to set more accurate customer expectations.

***Takeaway*:**

Maya's leadership wasn't about authority, it was about awareness, initiative, and problem-solving. By stepping back to see the bigger picture, she identified a systemic issue and implemented a structured solution that strengthened collaboration across teams. True leadership is not just about fixing what's broken today; it's about creating processes that drive long-term success.

3. Own the Narrative:

Strategic thinking isn't enough, you need to communicate effectively. When presenting your work, shift the focus from tasks completed to the outcomes achieved, the challenges overcome, and the broader value delivered. This not only positions you as a leader but also challenges perceptions that could limit your potential.

How to Own the Narrative:

- **Speak the Language of Impact**: Frame your work in terms of measurable results and business goals.
    - Instead of: *"I completed the market research report."*

- Say: *"The market research report identified three untapped opportunities, which could drive 20% growth in Q4 if pursued."*
- **Anticipate Follow-Up Questions**: Strategic leaders think beyond their role and consider organizational priorities. Be ready to answer questions like: *"What's next?"* or *"How does this support broader business goals?"*
- **Tie Your Success to the Team's Success**: Highlight how your work enables others, improves processes, or contributes to organizational wins.

Action Step: For every project or task, you complete, write down:

1. What was the outcome?
2. How did it align with or advance organization goals?
3. What opportunities for improvement or innovation did you uncover?

Example: Reframing the Narrative

Imagine you're a customer support lead responsible for handling escalations. You and your team resolve customer issues quickly, ensuring high satisfaction scores. That's great—but if you only frame your work around resolving tickets, leadership may see you as an effective problem-solver rather than a strategic driver of customer success.

Here's how to shift from task execution to strategic impact:

- **Task-Focused:**
  "I resolved 95% of escalations within 24 hours last quarter."

- **Strategic-Focused:**
  "By analyzing escalation trends, I identified a recurring product issue that led to 20% of support tickets. Working with the product team, we implemented a fix that reduced related escalations by 40%, improving customer retention."

By shifting the focus to insights, cross-functional collaboration, and business impact, you position yourself as a leader who improves processes, not just executes tasks.

Takeaway:

Instead of just tracking how many customer issues you solve, start looking at why they happen, how to prevent them, and how your insights can shape customer experience strategy. That's how you transition from *doing the work* to *guiding the work*.

Reflection Exercise

1. **Identify a Task You Completed Recently**: Write down what you did and the immediate result.
2. **Reframe It Strategically**:
   - What was the broader impact of your work?
   - How did it align with team or organization goals?
   - What challenges did you overcome to deliver it?
3. **Communicate It:** Craft a 1-2 sentence summary that highlights your strategic value and share it in your next team meeting, check-in, or performance review.

Bringing It Together

Transitioning from task execution to strategic thinking isn't about abandoning the skills that got you here. It's about **elevating how you think, act, and communicate your value**. This shift is essential for breaking through systemic barriers and redefining perceptions about your leadership potential.

When you begin asking bigger questions, connecting the dots, and owning the narrative, you position yourself not just as a "doer" but as a **driver of strategy and innovation**—a leader with the vision to create long-term impact.

Next Step: At your next meeting or project discussion, practice communicating your ideas through a strategic lens. Focus on outcomes, alignment, and opportunities for innovation. Your shift into leadership begins with how you frame your contributions.

Understanding the Difference Between Leading and Managing

The journey from managing processes to leading people is a defining moment in any career, but especially so us navigating corporate spaces. While management ensures systems and tasks are executed efficiently, leadership requires vision, influence, and the ability to inspire others toward a shared goal. This transition is often more complex - balancing the demands of delivering results with the unspoken responsibilities of representation, advocacy, and navigating systemic barriers.

Key Differences Between Managing and Leading

While management and leadership are interconnected, the distinction between the two is essential for professional growth:

Managers:
- Focus on **processes**, **deadlines**, and **tasks** to ensure day-to-day operations run smoothly.
- Solve **short-term problems**, prioritizing immediate deliverables and tactical solutions.
- Measure success through **output and efficiency**, ensuring goals are achieved on time and within scope.
- Maintain existing systems, processes, and structures.

Leaders:
- Focus on **people**, **vision**, and **long-term outcomes** to drive sustainable success.
- Empower teams to think creatively, innovate, and find solutions together.

- Measure success by **growth**, **influence**, and the team's ability to overcome challenges and achieve strategic goals.
- Inspire trust and foster environments where team members feel seen, valued, and motivated to do their best work.

Mindset Shift: Managers keep the ship afloat; leaders chart the course and inspire the crew to see the horizon.

Why This Transition Matters

Transitioning from managing to leading often comes with additional layers of complexity:

- **Proving Yourself Twice Over:** As a Black leader you may feel the need to constantly prove your competency—sometimes doing both management and leadership work simultaneously—just to be seen as "worthy" of advancement or even for your position.
- **Navigating Bias:** Bias can sometimes mean that you are valued more for your ability to "execute tasks" rather than for their strategic insights or leadership potential. Breaking through these perceptions requires visibility, advocacy, and a shift in how you position your contributions.
- **The Unspoken Role of Advocacy:** As a Black leader, you may find yourself naturally stepping into roles that others do not—advocate for equity, mentoring other Black professionals, or challenging systemic barriers. These additional responsibilities require a higher level of emotional intelligence, resilience, and vision.

Unique Leadership Opportunities

While there are challenges, stepping into leadership as a Black professional also presents a unique opportunity to redefine corporate culture, inspire change, and open doors for others:

1. **Advocating for Equity:** As a leader, you are able to challenge inequitable practices and policies. Whether it's questioning biased hiring processes, mentoring diverse talent, or advocating for equitable pay, your leadership can drive meaningful systemic change.
2. **Creating Safe Spaces:** You may often find yourself in environments where you feel isolated or overlooked. As a leader, you can create a culture where psychological safety, authenticity, and belonging are the norm—not the exception.
3. **Mentoring and Sponsoring Others:** Representation matters. By mentoring others who face similar barriers, you provide guidance and open pathways for future Black leaders. Sponsorship—actively advocating for someone's advancement—is particularly powerful in creating lasting change.
4. **Innovating with Unique Perspectives:** Your lived experiences equip you with perspectives that are often missing in corporate spaces. Lean into this strength—your creativity, critical thinking, and unique worldview can fuel innovative solutions and drive business results.

How to Shift from Managing to Leading

The transition from managing to leading requires more than a title change—it's a mindset shift. Here's how you can start:

1. **Empower Others to Solve Problems:**
   Instead of being the person who always "fixes it," challenge your team to find solutions. Ask questions like: *"How would you approach this problem?"* or *"What solutions can we explore together?"* This encourages ownership and builds confidence within your team.

2. **Delegate Strategically:**
   Managers often resist delegation because they fear tasks won't be done "right." Leaders trust their team, assign responsibilities based on strengths, and provide guidance rather than control. Focus on outcomes, not micromanaging processes.

3. **Articulate the Vision:**
   Leaders inspire people by helping them understand the "why." Whether leading a team, department, or initiative, communicate the broader vision and how each person contributes to it. This inspires alignment, engagement, and innovation.

4. **Shift to Coaching:**
   Leaders invest in developing people rather than managing tasks. Instead of giving directives, take on the role of a coach: ask questions, give constructive feedback, and help team members identify their strengths and growth opportunities.

5. **Prioritize Long-Term Impact:**
   Look beyond day-to-day deliverables and ask yourself:
   - "What strategic outcomes are we driving?"
   - "How can we innovate, streamline, or add value?"

- "What legacy am I building as a leader?"

Reflection: Am I Building a Culture Where Others Can Thrive?

Ask yourself these questions to assess your leadership approach:

- *Do I empower my team to take ownership of their work, or do I micromanage?*
- *How often do I align my team's tasks with long-term goals and vision?*
- *Am I fostering an inclusive and supportive environment where every team member feels valued and encouraged to grow?*
- *How can I step back from task execution to create opportunities for others to shine?*

Action Step: Write down three ways you can empower your team or peers this week. This could include delegating a project, mentoring a colleague, or creating space for others to share ideas in a meeting.

Example: **Leadership in Action**

Imagine being a mid-level professional managing a team where you've always been hands-on with execution. Your natural instinct is to fix problems quickly, but you recognize that this limits their ability to focus on strategy and team development.

- **Shift 1:** In your next project, instead of solving an issue alone, ask the team for solutions: *"How can we approach this differently to get the best outcome?"*
- **Shift 2:** During performance reviews, emphasize development: *"What skills would you like to strengthen, and how can I help you grow into your next role?"*

- **Shift 3:** Present the team's successes to leadership in a way that highlights long-term value: *"By empowering the team to lead, we reduced project timelines by 10% and uncovered new efficiencies."*

By shifting from task execution to vision-driven leadership, you not only elevate your role but also create opportunities for others.

The journey from managing to leading is a pivotal step in your career. This transition is about more than titles—it's about owning your influence, challenging systemic biases, and building a culture where you and others can thrive. Leadership requires vision, empowerment, and a focus on long-term outcomes.

Remember: You are not just here to "do the work." You are here to **guide the work, inspire the people, and lead with purpose**. *Your leadership matters—and the way you show up can transform your team, your organization, and the path for those who follow.*

Shifting Focus from "Doing the Work" to "Guiding the Work"

One of the hardest transitions especially for us, particularly when trust, visibility, and credibility are still being earned, is stepping back from executing every task to guiding others to do the work. Many of us have been taught that we must be "twice as good" to succeed, and as a result, we often overcompensate by trying to do everything ourselves. This "doer mindset" can become a double-edged sword: while it proves our capability, it also traps us in a cycle of individual contribution that limits our leadership potential.

In leadership, **your role is no longer about completing tasks, it's about empowering others to complete them well.** The transition from doing to guiding requires trust, intentional delegation, and a shift in how you define your value.

Why This Shift Is Critical

1. **Your Impact Is Limited When You Do It All**
   When you focus on doing the work, you may deliver excellent results, but your influence is limited to what you alone can achieve. High-performing leaders understand that their success is measured not by their individual contributions, but by their team's ability to thrive and deliver consistent results.

2. **Leadership Is About Multiplying Results**
   Guiding the work allows you to develop and empower your team to perform at their best. When you shift your focus to mentoring, delegating, and creating systems for success, you multiply your impact. This approach creates a ripple effect: you build a high-performing team

that not only meets goals but innovates and grows.

3. You Become a Better Strategic Thinker
Stepping away from execution creates space for strategic thinking. When you're consumed with the details, you miss the bigger picture. Leaders focus on outcomes, opportunities, and challenges—ensuring the team's work aligns with broader organizational goals.

4. Avoiding Burnout and Overwhelm
The pressure to over-deliver can lead to burnout. By holding on to tasks that could be delegated, you risk becoming overwhelmed, which diminishes your ability to lead effectively. Learning to let go and trust your team ensures you can sustain your energy for higher-level priorities.

5. Building Future Leaders
Great leaders don't just execute—they build other leaders. When you guide and empower your team, you create opportunities for others to shine, develop new skills, and prepare for leadership roles of their own. This is how you build a legacy of leadership that extends far beyond your individual contributions.

How to Guide the Work Effectively

1. Delegate with Purpose
Delegation is not about dumping tasks on your team, it's about entrusting them with meaningful responsibilities that allow them to grow and contribute.

- **Identify the Right Tasks:** Start by evaluating your workload and asking: *"What tasks require* my leadership, and what tasks can I empower others to handle?"

- **Choose the Right People:** Assign tasks to team members based on their strengths, interests (when appropriate), and areas for development. Delegation is an opportunity to invest in your team's growth.
- **Provide Context and Clarity:** Set clear expectations for the task, including its purpose, goals, and deadlines. Give team members the tools, resources, support and autonomy they need to succeed.
- **Trust and Step Back:** Let go of the urge to micromanage. Allow your team to approach the work in their own way. Keep in mind that mistakes will happen, but regular check-ins can mitigate the impact of most missteps, and you can present them as learning opportunities.

Example Situation: As a customer success manager, you were managing high-value client accounts while also handling onboarding for new customers. You were stretched thin, and response times were slipping.

Task: You needed to ensure that onboarding was handled effectively without personally overseeing every new customer setup.

Action: You assigned a senior team member to lead onboarding and provided them with a structured checklist, FAQs, and escalation guidelines. You held weekly check-ins to address challenges and reinforce key goals.

Result: Not only did the onboarding process become more efficient, but the senior team member gained confidence in leading. Over three months, onboarding times improved by 20%, and customer satisfaction scores increased by 15%.

Lesson: Mistakes happened in the early weeks, but regular check-ins helped adjust the approach and turn missteps into learning opportunities.

2. Share the Vision

Teams are more motivated and engaged when they understand the bigger picture. As a leader, it's your responsibility to connect the dots and help your team see why their work matters.

- **Communicate the "Why":** Don't just tell your team *what* to do—explain *why* it matters. Help them see how their contributions align with team, departmental, or organizational goals.
- **Paint the Big Picture:** Share the long-term vision and outcomes you're working toward. Inspire your team by showing them how their work contributes to something greater.
- **Involve Your Team:** Invite input and ideas from your team to foster a sense of ownership. When people feel invested in the outcome, they bring more creativity and accountability to their work.

***Example Situation*:** A new initiative was introduced to reduce customer churn, but the team saw it as just another checklist item rather than a strategic priority. Engagement was low.

Task: You needed to make sure the team understood why this initiative mattered and how their role contributed to the bigger picture.

Action: In your next team meeting, instead of just rolling out the steps, you connected the initiative to real customer impact. You shared data on churn rates, played a clip of customer feedback, and explained how their efforts could improve retention. You then set a clear goal and recognized team members who were already applying best practices.

Result: Within three months, customer retention among at-risk accounts improved by 12%, and engagement with the initiative increased as team members felt more invested.

Lesson: Some team members initially resisted the change, but one-on-one conversations helped them see the value and get on board.

3. Support Without Micromanaging

Supporting your team means being present, providing guidance, and removing obstacles—but not doing the work for them. Trust is key to effective leadership.

- **Be Available for Guidance:** Let your team know they can come to you for support when needed. Schedule regular check-ins to discuss progress, challenges, and ideas.
- **Focus on Outcomes, Not Methods:** Allow team members to approach tasks in their own way as long as they achieve the desired outcome. This fosters creativity and builds confidence.
- **Remove Barriers:** Identify obstacles—whether they're resource gaps, unclear priorities, or interpersonal conflicts—and work to resolve them so your team can perform their best.

Example Situation: A company-wide shift introduced a new customer support ticketing system designed to improve response times and streamline workflows. However, the team struggled with adoption, with some members reverting to old methods and others expressing frustration with the learning curve.

Task: You needed to support the team in adapting to the new system without micromanaging or constantly stepping in to correct mistakes.

Action: Instead of checking every ticket or hovering over team members, you created a structured but flexible approach to support the transition. You scheduled a team discussion to address concerns, allowing members to share challenges and propose solutions. To build confidence, you identified key features that could immediately benefit their daily work and demonstrated quick wins rather than overwhelming them with the entire system. You encouraged peer learning by having those who adapted quickly share their best practices. Rather than monitoring every interaction, you implemented biweekly check-ins where team members could troubleshoot challenges together and discuss improvements.

Result: Within six weeks, system adoption improved by 85%, and response times decreased by 20% as team members became more comfortable with the new workflows. Additionally, overall satisfaction with the system improved as employees felt heard and involved in refining the process.

Lesson: Some mistakes happened early on, but allowing space for problem-solving and regular check-ins helped mitigate them without creating a culture of over-supervision.

Letting Go of Perfectionism

As a Black professional, the pressure to be "twice as good" often manifests as perfectionism. The belief that every task must be flawless can make it difficult to delegate or trust others. However, perfectionism can hold you back as a leader by preventing you from focusing on higher-level responsibilities. Striving for excellence is valuable, but if you let the fear of mistakes—especially how they might be perceived or used against you—dictate your actions, you'll hold yourself back. The reality is that mistakes will happen, and sometimes, they will be scrutinized unfairly. The key is to stay in control of your own narrative and use those moments to reinforce—not diminish—your leadership.

Reframe Perfectionism as Growth:

- Understand that mistakes are part of the learning process. Empower your team to take risks, make mistakes, and grow.
- Recognize that leadership is not about being perfect, it's about enabling progress. Your role is to guide, support, and inspire.
- Trust that your team will rise to the occasion when given responsibility and autonomy.
- Mistakes may be held against you but you can use them to your advantage.

Example: **Leading a Major Project**

You were leading a major process improvement initiative that was meant to streamline workflows across multiple teams. Despite thorough planning, an oversight in implementation caused delays, and leadership was frustrated. While others on the team made similar missteps, your mistake was singled out in a leadership meeting, and it was clear that the blame was falling disproportionately on you.

In that moment, the instinct might be to over-explain, go on the defensive, or retreat into self-doubt. Instead, you took control of the situation. You acknowledged the mistake, but you didn't allow it to define the entire project. You calmly laid out the adjustments that had already been made, how the issue had been corrected, and what long-term improvements had come from it. You also reminded the group of the broader wins the initiative had already delivered—faster response times, reduced errors, and a more efficient workflow. Rather than letting the mistake become the headline, you reframed the discussion around problem-solving, accountability, and progress.

A possible result? The conversation shifted. While the criticism didn't disappear, it was clear you were not flustered or shaken. Over time, that moment didn't stick as a failure—it became an example of your ability to lead through challenges.

Takeaway:

Some people will weaponize mistakes, but how you respond determines the lasting impact. If you accept responsibility, pivot to solutions, and maintain composure, you send a clear message: your leadership is defined by resilience, not by a single misstep.

Exercises: Shifting Into a Leadership Mindset

Exercise 1: From Execution to Strategy

To get the most out of these exercises, choose a single team or project you are currently working on. This consistency will help you see the full picture—how your role can shift from execution to strategy, how leadership differs from management, and how delegation plays a role in that transition.

Think about your role in this project or team. List the tasks you are responsible for completing. Now, step back and ask yourself:

- Are you focused more on executing tasks or shaping the overall direction?
- What strategic insights can you bring that would improve the long-term success of this project?
- How can you connect this work to broader organizational goals?

Write down one way you can shift your focus from execution to a more strategic perspective.

Exercise 2: Leadership vs. Management

Using the same project or team, analyze how you currently operate:

- When challenges arise, do you focus on solving the immediate issue (management) or coaching the team to develop long-term solutions (leadership)?
- Do you tend to give instructions and monitor execution, or do you empower your team to take ownership of outcomes?

- Are you focused on maintaining processes, or are you looking ahead to drive improvements and innovation?

Write down one leadership shift you can make in how you approach this project.

Exercise 3: Delegation in Action

Still using the same project or team, look at your workload:
- What are you holding onto that someone else could take on?
- What's preventing you from delegating—trust, time, or the belief that you can do it better?
- If you had to free up 20% of your time to focus on strategy, what would you delegate first?

Now, pick one task to delegate and outline how you will provide guidance without micromanaging.

Shifting from "doing the work" to "guiding the work" is not about stepping back—it's about stepping up. By empowering others, communicating a clear vision, and letting go of perfectionism, you position yourself as a leader capable of driving outcomes at scale. This shift is critical for your growth as a leader and for building a team that thrives under your guidance.

Conclusion

Transitioning into leadership is more than a title or a list of new responsibilities, it's about embracing a new mindset. This shift requires navigating unique challenges, including pushing past stereotypes, overcoming bias, and knowing that you belong in spaces where strategic decisions are made. This is not about proving your worth through overwork or perfection—it's about owning your value and repositioning yourself as a visionary leader who drives long-term impact.

Leadership is not about doing more, it's about enabling others to achieve more. By stepping back from execution and shifting your focus to strategy, vision, and empowerment, you multiply your impact and create opportunities for others to thrive. When you guide the work instead of doing it all yourself, you're not stepping away, you're stepping up.

This shift is liberating. It allows you to move beyond the limiting role of "the doer" and into the role of a leader who inspires, empowers, and innovates. True leadership means trusting your team, connecting the dots others miss, and building an environment where success is shared. You don't have to carry it all alone—your greatest strength is your ability to guide others to their full potential.

As you embrace this new mindset, remember you belong here. Your strategic thinking, lived experience, and authentic leadership are assets that will propel you—and those you lead—forward.

Next Up: Learn how to build influence and visibility without compromising your identity or authenticity

Chapter 3: Staying Authentic in the Corporate Arena

Navigating corporate spaces as a Black professional often feels like walking a tightrope. On one side lies the desire to show up as your full, authentic self—embracing your culture, voice, and values. On the other side, there's the pressure to "fit in," to meet unspoken and sometimes ever-changing expectations about how you should speak, dress, act, or lead. It's no secret that corporate environments have historically been shaped by a narrow view of "professionalism", one that frequently sidelines or suppresses diversity.

For many of us, the tension is constant: *Do I blend in to be "accepted", or do I risk standing out to stay true to myself?* This struggle often leads to **code-switching**—the practice of altering your speech, behavior, or appearance to conform to the dominant culture. While code-switching can feel like a survival mechanism, it can come at a significant cost: eroding your sense of identity, increasing stress, and stifling your ability to lead with confidence and authenticity.

But here's the truth: You don't have to trade your authenticity for success. Staying true to yourself doesn't mean disregarding workplace "professionalism" (I put it in quotes because many corporate professionalisms are based in whiteness as a default); it means redefining professionalism on your terms. By embracing your unique voice, perspective, and values, you can thrive in corporate spaces without compromising who you are. This chapter provides practical strategies to resist code-switching, navigate biases, and show up as the authentic leader you're meant to be.

Strategies to Resist Code-Switching (Hint: It Has Nothing to Do with Professionalism)

Code-switching—whether it's changing your tone, hairstyle, word choices, or cultural references—can feel like a way to protect yourself in environments where you fear being misunderstood, judged, or excluded. While it's often done out of necessity, the long-term impact can be draining. Constantly monitoring and adjusting yourself to fit someone else's standard is mentally and emotionally exhausting. Worse, it can make you feel like your success is dependent on hiding parts of yourself.

Staying authentic doesn't mean rejecting "professionalism"; it means refusing to shrink or contort yourself to meet someone else's idea of what professionalism looks like. Your identity, culture, and lived experiences are assets, not liabilities. Let's break the cycle and explore strategies that allow you to show up as your best, most authentic self:

<u>Set Boundaries Early and Clearly</u>

Staying authentic begins with setting clear boundaries that honor your values and priorities. This is not about explaining yourself to others but about communicating who you are, what you need, and how you work best.

Why This Matters:

Boundaries create a sense of agency. When you define how you show up, others are more likely to respect and value you for who you are. Don't forget that boundaries are for you, and no one is obligated to respect them except for you. So, if others do not respect your boundaries, you have the responsibility to act accordingly.

Examples of Setting Boundaries:

- If you need time for prayer, cultural practices, or family obligations, share this respectfully and confidently. For example:
  "I prioritize Friday afternoons for prayer and reflection. I'll be unavailable during that time but happy to support before or after."
- If microaggressions or coded feedback arise (e.g., comments about "tone" or "professionalism"), address them calmly but firmly:
  "I appreciate the feedback, and I always aim to communicate effectively. Can you clarify what you mean by 'tone'? I want to ensure we're aligned on substance rather than style."

My Story

For years, I felt like I had to "turn on" for work. I regulated my tone, adjusted my pitch, and kept a constant smile on my face—not because it felt natural, but because I believed it was the only way to avoid being perceived as aggressive. Every interaction required careful calibration, and over time, it became physically and mentally exhausting.

One day, I made a decision: I was done performing. Instead of filtering myself to fit a mold, I chose to walk and talk in my confidence. I spoke with conviction, held my head high, and refused to shrink myself to make others comfortable. The response? I was told that I had a "commanding presence" when I entered a room—though it was not meant as a compliment. But I decided to take it as one. Their perception of me didn't change, but my perception of myself did, and that mattered far more.

Tip: Setting boundaries is not just about external expectations, it's about internal alignment. When you decide to show up as your full, authentic self, others may resist, but the real power lies in how *you* feel about you. Authenticity is not about changing how the world sees you; it's about standing firm in how you see yourself.

Find Allies Who Value and Celebrate Authenticity

You don't have to navigate this journey alone. Building relationships with people who value diversity and equity creates a network of support and safety—people who not only *see* your authenticity but actively encourage it.

What Allies Do:

- Amplify your voice in meetings and spaces where you may feel overlooked.
- Offer guidance and mentorship based on their own experiences navigating authenticity in corporate environments.
- Create opportunities for you to shine and support you when challenges arise.

How to Find Allies:

- Seek out leaders, peers, or mentors who value equity and celebrate diverse voices. This could include connecting with Employee Resource Groups (ERGs) or external professional organizations.

- Foster reciprocal relationships by being an ally to others. Show up for colleagues who are also striving to bring their full selves to work.

Tip: Don't underestimate the value of mentorship and sponsorship from those who understand the challenges of balancing authenticity and success. Allies can be key to helping you navigate difficult conversations and stay grounded in your identity.

Lead by Example: Authenticity Breeds Authenticity

Authenticity is contagious. When you show up as your true self—whether it's in how you lead, communicate, or express your cultural identity—you create a ripple effect that inspires others to do the same. This is particularly powerful when you're in a leadership role: your authenticity gives permission for others to be themselves, fostering trust, belonging, and innovation within your team.

Ways to Lead Authentically:

- **Share Your Story:** Use opportunities to speak about your journey, challenges, and values. This builds connection and demonstrates vulnerability—a hallmark of authentic leadership.
- **Be Consistent:** Align your words, actions, and values. People respect leaders who are genuine and unwavering in their integrity.
- **Celebrate Diversity:** Create an environment where cultural differences are embraced, not minimized. Encourage team members to share their unique perspectives, traditions, and ideas.

Tip: Authentic leadership is not about perfection. It's about showing up consistently, creating safe space for others, and proving that success doesn't require erasing who you are.

Redefining Professionalism: It's About Integrity, Not Conformity

Too often, professionalism is weaponized to exclude people who don't fit a narrow mold. For many of us, this can mean facing unfair critiques about tone, appearance, and/or communication style. But professionalism isn't about conforming to someone else's standard—it's about delivering results with integrity, respect, and excellence.

What Professionalism *Really* Looks Like:
- Showing up prepared, reliable, and engaged.
- Communicating clearly, respectfully, and effectively.
- Delivering results, solving problems, and adding value to your organization.

What professionalism does *not* require is sacrificing your identity, culture, or voice. When you redefine professionalism on your terms, you stop seeking external validation from others and start showing up with confidence, clarity, and purpose.

Key Takeaway

Staying authentic in corporate spaces is not easy—it's an act of courage and resistance. While code-switching may feel like a short-term survival strategy, the long-term cost may be too high. By setting boundaries, finding allies, and leading by example, you can redefine what success and professionalism looks like for you. Remember, authenticity is not a barrier to success; it's a superpower that sets you apart and allows you to lead with impact.

Ask Yourself:
- *What parts of myself do I feel pressured to hide at work and why?*
- *How can I redefine professionalism so that it aligns with my values and identity?*
- *Who are my allies, and how can I lean on them to stay authentic in challenging spaces?*

Your authenticity is your greatest strength. The corporate world needs your voice, your perspective, and your leadership—not a watered-down version of who you are. Show up as your full self and inspire others to do the same.

Navigating Microaggressions and Addressing Bias with Confidence

Microaggressions—those subtle, sometimes unintentional slights rooted in bias—can feel like a constant undercurrent in the corporate world, especially for us. They are more than just "small" moments. They are **exhausting**, accumulating overtime and chipping away at your sense of belonging, confidence, and emotional well-being.

From the moment you experience a microaggression, the weight of it begins: **Did that just happen?** Then comes the mental calculus—**Should I say something? Will it make things worse? Will I be labeled difficult or overly sensitive?** This decision-making process itself is draining, especially when we know that even addressing the issue can lead to backlash, defensiveness, or gaslighting.

Let's be real: Navigating microaggressions is a burden we shouldn't have to carry. But since we do, we need tools that balance our emotional well-being with our ability to advocate for ourselves. The following steps are designed to be impactful but realistic—so you're not constantly using up your energy fighting battles that shouldn't exist in the first place.

Steps to Navigate Microaggressions (Without Losing Yourself in the Process)

1. Pause and Assess

Before responding, take a moment to check in with yourself. Not every microaggression requires immediate confrontation, and **not every battle is worth your energy**.

Ask yourself:
- Was this an isolated incident or part of a larger pattern?
- Do I have the energy to address this right now?
- Will speaking up create meaningful change, or will it lead to more frustration?
- Can I protect my peace while still holding this person accountable?

Remember, **intent does not erase impact**. Even if the microaggression wasn't malicious, the harm it causes is still real and valid. If this is a one-time comment from someone who seems open to feedback, addressing it might be worth it. But if this is a pattern, you might need to document it or escalate it strategically. **Your well-being comes first.**

Example: If someone interrupts you repeatedly in a meeting, pause to assess whether addressing it in the moment will help reset the dynamic or whether following up privately will be more impactful.

2. Speak with Clarity (If You Choose to Engage)

If you decide to address the microaggression, be **direct but measured**. Keep the focus on the impact, not the person's intent (because "I didn't mean it that way" will likely be their first defense).

Use clear, non-apologetic language:

"I noticed that my point wasn't acknowledged until someone else repeated it. I want to make sure my contributions are recognized in real time."

"You've called me by another Black colleague's name a few times. I want to make sure you know my name is [your name]."

"I want to clarify something—you mentioned my tone, but I'd like to understand what specifically felt off to you."

Why This Matters:

You are **naming the issue** without giving them space to dismiss it. You are **not apologizing** or softening your words to make them comfortable. You are setting a boundary without inviting a debate over whether the offense "was meant that way." **And if they get defensive?** Let them. Your job is to stand firm, not to manage their emotions.

3. Document Patterns (CYA)

Document, Document. Document, I'll say it again, document everything, regardless if microaggressions are frequent, it's important to document them. This not only helps you process what's happening but also provides evidence if you need to escalate the issue to HR or management. This may be happening to others that you are unaware of particularly if this comes from people that you may not have regular contact with.

What to Document:
- The date, time, and location of the incident.
- A brief description of what was said or done and the context.
- Any witnesses who were present.
- How it made you feel or impacted your work.

Why This Matters:

If it happens again, you have receipts to show it's not isolated. If you escalate to HR or leadership, you're coming with facts, not feelings (because HR cares about patterns, not one-off complaints). It helps you recognize when to let something go versus when it's becoming a workplace issue.

Tip: If you're unsure whether to escalate, review your documentation after a few weeks. If you see a clear pattern, it's time to take action.

4. Engage in Dialogue (When It Feels Worth It)

In one-on-one settings, consider using dialogue as a tool for education. Many people are unaware of how their words or actions perpetuate bias, and a constructive conversation can be a learning opportunity.

How to Start the Conversation:

"I wanted to bring something to your attention—when you [describe behavior], it came across as [explain impact]."

- "I know this might not have been your intention, but I want to make you aware of how this landed on my end."
- "Going forward, I'd appreciate it if you [suggest alternative behavior]."

If they seem **open to learning**, great. But if they get defensive or dismissive, **stop engaging**—you've done your part.

- **Tips for Effective Dialogue:**

  - Focus on the behavior, not the person.
  - Be specific about what happened and the impact it had.

Offer a constructive perspective: "In the future, I'd appreciate it if you [suggest alternative behavior]."

When Dialogue Isn't Productive:
Not every person will be open to feedback, and that's okay. If you encounter resistance, remember that your worth is not tied to someone else's ability to learn. Escalate the issue if needed, and be sure to document the conversation regardless if it was productive or not so that you have a paper trail.

And **when dialogue isn't productive**? Move to **Protect Your Energy**.

The Mental Toll of Microaggressions: Protecting Your Energy

This is the part that often gets ignored: **Addressing microaggressions takes a toll on us.** The emotional labor of constantly defending your presence, worth, or professionalism is draining. Some days, you simply won't have the energy to fight, and that's okay.

Here's how to protect your mental and emotional well-being:

- **Lean on Allies** – Find colleagues, mentors, or friends who understand the weight of what you're dealing with. Even just venting to someone who "gets it" can be healing.
- **Know When to Escalate** – If microaggressions are persistent, targeted, or escalating into a toxic work environment, **HR needs to be involved.** Protect your peace before it affects your performance, reputation, or job satisfaction.
- **Take Breaks** – If work is feeling like a battle every day, step away when possible. A walk, a mental reset, or a "Do Not Disturb" hour can help **recenter you**.
- **Give Yourself Permission to Let Some Things Go** – Some days, silence is self-care. You don't have to fight every battle—choose the ones that matter most.

By Addressing Microaggressions, You Can Create Change

When you push back against microaggressions, you're not just standing up for yourself, you're setting the expectation that **respect is the standard**.

But let's be clear: **It is not your job to fix corporate culture alone.** Do what you can, when you can, but **never at the expense of your peace.**

Reflection:

- When was the last time you experienced a microaggression at work? How did it affect you?
- What's one strategy from this list you can use next time?
- How can you better protect your emotional energy while still advocating for yourself?

Your presence in the workplace is valid, necessary, and valuable. **Let no one make you feel otherwise.**

Personal Stories of Black Leaders Who Thrived Authentically

Authenticity in corporate spaces isn't just an ideal - it's a proven strategy for success. While the pressure to conform is real, the stories of Black leaders who embraced their identity demonstrate that authenticity can be a powerful driver of innovation, influence, and leadership impact.

Here are some examples of Black leaders who thrived by staying true to themselves and using their unique perspectives to drive change:

Case Study 1: David, The Career Catalyst (Finding an Ally Who Supported Career Growth)

David, a rising finance professional, was consistently exceeding expectations, yet he struggled to gain visibility for high-impact projects. His contributions were often overlooked in leadership discussions, and promotions seemed to go to colleagues with similar or lesser experience. Frustrated but determined, he sought guidance.

David found an unexpected ally in a senior executive, a white woman who had noticed his strong analytical skills and leadership potential. Instead of simply offering encouragement, she became an **active sponsor**—advocating for him in rooms he wasn't in. She pushed for his inclusion in major projects, coached him on navigating corporate politics, and made sure leadership recognized his value.

With her support, David not only earned a leadership role but also built the confidence to advocate for himself. Over time, he paid it forward—mentoring other underrepresented professionals and ensuring his team fostered a culture of sponsorship and inclusion.

Outcome: With the backing of an ally who used her influence effectively, David's career trajectory shifted. His promotion led to a seat at decision-making tables, where he now ensures diverse talent is seen, heard, and valued.

Key Takeaway: An ally isn't just someone who says they support you—they take action. Finding someone willing to advocate for your growth can be a game-changer in a system where hard work alone isn't always enough.

Case Study 2: Nina, The Authentic Leader (Authenticity Breeds Authenticity by Redefining Professionalism)

Nina, a senior HR director, had spent years code-switching—altering her speech, toning down her natural expressions, and avoiding cultural references to fit the unspoken corporate mold of "professionalism." But over time, she grew tired of the exhausting performance and made a decision to lead on her own terms.

She stopped straightening her hair for the sake of "polish" and started wearing her natural curls. She used her real voice in meetings—direct, warm, and expressive—rather than softening it to avoid being seen as aggressive. Most importantly, she challenged outdated views of professionalism within her company.

When leadership questioned whether a Black employee's locs were "appropriate" for a customer-facing role, Nina shut it down immediately, presenting research on workplace bias and pointing out that professionalism is about competence, not conformity. Under her leadership, the company revamped its dress code and grooming policies to explicitly prohibit race-based discrimination.

Outcome: Nina's authenticity didn't just empower

her—it shifted company culture. Her visibility encouraged other employees to bring their full selves to work, creating an environment where authenticity was embraced rather than tolerated.

Key Takeaway: Redefining professionalism starts with showing up as yourself. When you lead authentically, you create space for others to do the same—and ultimately, challenge biased systems that equate whiteness with excellence.

Case Study 3: Jordan, The Unshaken Professional (Handling Microaggressions with Confidence)

Jordan, a high-performing project manager, was no stranger to microaggressions. From being mistaken for a junior employee to being told he was "so articulate" as if it were surprising, he had learned to navigate these moments with patience. But one incident forced him to take a stand.

During a leadership meeting, a colleague interrupted him multiple times, only for another team member to repeat his exact idea moments later—this time met with nods of approval. It wasn't the first time this had happened, but Jordan decided it would be the last.

Instead of letting it slide, he calmly spoke up: *"I actually just shared that point a moment ago. I'd love to hear your thoughts on how we can build on it."*

The room went silent for a moment, then leadership acknowledged Jordan's original contribution. After the meeting, the interrupter awkwardly apologized, claiming it wasn't intentional. Jordan didn't need the apology—he needed the behavior to change.

To prevent future incidents, Jordan began documenting patterns of dismissive behavior in meetings.

He also built relationships with allies who started reinforcing his contributions in real time— "As Jordan just mentioned…"—to ensure credit was given where it was due.

Outcome: Speaking up in the moment changed the dynamic. Over time, Jordan noticed fewer interruptions, and his ideas were acknowledged without needing to be echoed by someone else first. His calm but firm response set a standard for how he expected to be treated moving forward.

Key Takeaway: Microaggressions thrive in silence. Addressing them head-on, while exhausting, sets boundaries that protect your confidence and professional reputation.

Lessons from These Stories

These stories share a common thread: **authenticity, advocacy, and strategic action**. These leaders didn't just survive corporate spaces—they thrived by leveraging their unique perspectives, finding support, and challenging bias.

What We Can Learn from Them:

1. **Sponsorship Changes Careers:** David's story proves that having an active ally who advocates for your success can open doors that hard work alone sometimes can't.
2. **Authenticity Redefines Professionalism:** Nina showed that being yourself isn't just liberating—it's leadership. When you stop code-switching, you empower others to do the same and shift workplace culture in the process.
3. **Setting Boundaries Changes Perceptions:** Jordan's approach to handling microaggressions proves that holding people accountable, even

subtly, forces them to do better—and signals to others that you won't be overlooked.

Your Turn: Embrace Authenticity as an Asset
Reflect:
- What aspects of your identity or culture have you felt pressured to minimize at work and why do you feel pressured?
- Have you experienced the power of sponsorship or advocacy? If not, what steps can you take to find an ally?

Act:
- How can you use your authenticity to empower others in your workplace?
- What's one microaggression or bias you want to challenge moving forward?

Your **authenticity** isn't just a personal strength, it's a **leadership asset**. When you embrace it fully, you create space for others to thrive alongside you.

Conclusion

Corporate spaces often pressure us to conform, to shrink ourselves into versions that feel "palatable" to the dominant culture. But here's the truth: **your authenticity is your superpower.** It's not a liability to be managed; it's an asset to be leveraged. Staying true to yourself, even in the face of microaggressions, bias, and systemic challenges, requires a unique combination of confidence, clarity, and resilience.

When you embrace your identity as a source of strength, you begin to redefine what it means to succeed in corporate spaces. You create room for innovation by bringing new perspectives to the table. You challenge the status quo simply by existing authentically. And you inspire others, both colleagues and future leaders—by showing that success doesn't require abandoning who you are.

Key Takeaways:

1. Authenticity doesn't mean sacrificing professionalism, it means redefining it in a way that aligns with your values.
2. Addressing bias and microaggressions isn't just about self-advocacy—it's about paving the way for more inclusive environments.
3. Leading authentically empowers others to do the same, creating a ripple effect of change that transforms corporate spaces.

Looking Ahead:

The next step is translating your authenticity into influence and visibility. How do you ensure your voice is heard and your contributions recognized, all while staying true to yourself?

As we move into the next chapter, you'll learn the art of building influence, cultivating relationships, and positioning yourself as a leader who thrives on authenticity.

Remember: **Your authenticity isn't just a part of your journey—it's the foundation of your leadership legacy**.

Chapter 4: Innovation Through Creativity

Leveraging Your Unique Perspective to Solve Problems in New Ways

Innovation is often framed as a tool for product development or groundbreaking technology, but it's just as critical to leadership. When navigating corporate spaces, your unique perspective isn't just a differentiator, it's a strength that can redefine how problems are solved.

Your lived experiences, cultural knowledge, and distinct insights provide you with the ability to see solutions others might overlook. While many companies claim to value "thinking outside the box," the truth is that traditional corporate cultures can stifle creativity, especially when it comes from voices that challenge the status quo. By leaning into your perspective, you can shift that narrative and demonstrate how diversity of thought drives impactful results.

Strategies for Leveraging Your Unique Perspective

Shift Your Mindset: Reframe Your Experiences as Assets

One of the most significant barriers to leveraging your perspective is the conditioning that often makes Black professionals question whether their viewpoints are "valid" or "professional" enough. It's time to dismantle that mindset.

- Recognize that your background brings a fresh lens to existing challenges. Whether it's growing up in a tight-knit community that taught you how to navigate relationships or overcoming systemic barriers that honed your resilience, these experiences equip you with skills that traditional corporate environments often undervalue.
- Instead of seeing differences as a disadvantage, embrace them as a competitive advantage. Your perspective allows you to see gaps and opportunities others miss.

Example: Consider a team tasked with improving employee engagement. While others may focus solely on financial incentives, your lived experience might lead you to suggest initiatives that address inclusion, psychological safety, or mentorship—elements that resonate deeply with underrepresented groups and drive engagement in more sustainable ways.

Ask the Right Questions to Challenge the Status Quo

Innovation begins with curiosity. The most groundbreaking ideas often stem from asking questions that others shy away from—questions that disrupt assumptions and force people to think differently.

- Shift from *"How do we fix this problem?"* to *"Why does this problem exist in the first place?"*
- Challenge existing frameworks by asking:
    - *"What if we approached this differently?"*
    - *"Who benefits from this current system, and who doesn't?"*
    - *"How does this solution work for people with different experiences, needs, or perspectives?"*

Example: In a discussion about product design, you might ask, *"How does this feature serve customers in underrepresented communities?"* or *"What would this process look like if accessibility were our top priority?"* These questions not only highlight blind spots but also create opportunities for more inclusive, impactful solutions.

Cross-Pollinate Ideas from Different Parts of Your Life

Innovation doesn't happen in isolation—it thrives when ideas collide. By drawing inspiration from diverse aspects of your life, you can introduce creative solutions that others may not consider.

- Think about the lessons you've learned from your community, hobbies, or cultural heritage. How do they apply to workplace challenges?
- Break down silos by connecting seemingly unrelated concepts. For example, lessons from community organizing—such as collaboration, resilience, and trust-building—can revolutionize approaches to team management or customer engagement.

Example: A professional with experience in grassroots activism might apply principles of community engagement to corporate strategy by proposing initiatives that involve stakeholders early and foster collaboration, rather than top-down directives.

Build Bridges Between Culture and Corporate Goals

Your cultural knowledge isn't just personal, it's a leadership tool. Use it to reimagine how problems are approached, and solutions are implemented.

- Incorporate cultural insights to better connect with diverse audiences, whether they're customers, employees, or stakeholders.
- Highlight the business case for diversity-driven innovation by showing how inclusive approaches drive better results. Remember that data matters.

Example: A senior consultant at a global firm noticed that their company's market research consistently overlooked insights from Black and Latino communities, leading to ineffective campaigns and missed revenue opportunities. Rather than treating this as a side issue, they leveraged their cultural knowledge to show leadership why these gaps mattered. They gathered data on the growing purchasing power of underrepresented demographics and presented case studies on brands that had successfully tapped into these markets. Then, they worked with cross-functional teams to develop a new research framework that incorporated culturally relevant insights, ensuring that future campaigns resonated authentically. The result was a marketing approach that not only increased engagement among diverse consumers but also led to a 20% revenue boost in previously untapped markets. By positioning cultural awareness as a business growth strategy, rather than just a diversity initiative, they proved that inclusion isn't just about optics—it's about impact.

Why Leveraging Your Perspective Builds Leadership Credibility

- **Innovative Problem-Solving:** When you offer solutions that challenge traditional thinking, you establish yourself as a forward-thinker who adds unique value to the organization.
- **Enhanced Team Dynamics:** Your ability to connect with people from diverse backgrounds fosters collaboration and inclusion, which are essential to high-performing teams. *You don't need to know everything.*
- **A Trusted Voice:** Leaders who bring their full selves to work—without compromising their authenticity—gain respect and influence, positioning themselves as role models for others navigating similar challenges.

Action Steps for Leveraging Your Perspective

1. **Identify a Workplace Challenge:** Think of a current issue your team or organization is facing. Reflect on how your unique background or insights might provide a new way to approach it.
2. **Frame Your Perspective Strategically:** Present your ideas in a way that aligns with organizational goals, highlighting how they drive value or solve critical problems.
3. **Advocate for Inclusive Solutions:** Be intentional about suggesting approaches that consider diverse experiences and perspectives, even if they challenge the status quo.

Your perspective is your power. While corporate spaces may not always recognize its value initially, consistently demonstrating how your unique insights drive innovation will build your credibility and expand your influence. Remember, innovation isn't about fitting in—it's about standing out and showing others what's possible when you embrace your full self.

Strategies to Present Unconventional Ideas in Traditional Spaces

Presenting unconventional ideas in corporate settings is often a balancing act. On one hand, you want to push boundaries and introduce fresh perspectives; on the other, you're navigating spaces that may default to tried-and-true methods. For many of us, this task can feel even more complex when your ideas challenge the dominant culture or status quo. However, with a strategic approach, you can transform hesitation into opportunity and position yourself as a forward-thinking leader.

Unconventional ideas thrive when they are presented with clarity, confidence, and alignment to organizational priorities (having the data to support you is even better). Let's explore practical strategies for sharing your vision and gaining buy-in, even in traditional spaces.

Steps to Present Ideas Effectively
1. Frame Your Idea with Data and Research

Facts speak louder than opinions, especially in corporate environments where stakeholders may need convincing to venture outside their comfort zones. Strengthen your proposal by grounding it in data, case studies, or real-world examples.

- **Use Quantitative Data:** Metrics, research studies, and benchmarks can lend credibility to your idea and show that it's not just a "wild idea" but a well-considered strategy.
- **Incorporate Qualitative Insights:** Testimonials, employee feedback, or anecdotal evidence can provide a human element that resonates with decision-makers.

Example: Proposing a leadership accelerator program for underrepresented employees? Back it up with retention data showing that diverse talent often leaves due to a lack of growth opportunities. Highlight industry research proving that companies with robust leadership pipelines are more profitable. Pair this with internal survey results where employees express a desire for structured career development. The combination of hard data and personal insights makes the case undeniable.

2. Align Your Idea with Organizational Goals

No matter how innovative your idea is, it will gain traction only if it addresses a specific pain point or aligns with your company's mission, vision, and values.

- **Link to Business Objectives:** Show how your idea supports revenue growth, efficiency, customer satisfaction, or employee engagement.
- **Use the Company's Language:** Reframe your idea using the organization's priorities and goals. For example, if your company values innovation, emphasize how your idea fosters creativity and strategic advantage.

Example: Proposing a supplier diversity initiative? Don't just frame it as an equity effort—connect it to business growth. Show how increasing contracts with minority-owned suppliers fosters innovation, strengthens corporate social responsibility, and aligns with consumer demand for ethical sourcing. Reference data from major corporations that have successfully implemented similar initiatives, demonstrating how it contributed to long-term profitability.

3. Utilize Storytelling to Build Connection

Stories are powerful tools for persuasion. They humanize your idea, making it relatable and easier for others to understand and support.

- **Start with a Personal Connection:** Share why this idea matters to you or how you've seen it succeed in the past.
- **Create an Emotional Hook:** Use an anecdote or scenario to illustrate the problem your idea solves or the impact it could have.
- **Visualize the Outcome:** Paint a vivid picture of how your idea could transform a process, team, or outcome.

Example: Pitching a mental health initiative for employees? Instead of just listing statistics, share the story of an industry peer whose company implemented similar programs, leading to lower burnout rates and higher retention. Then, walk decision-makers through a future scenario where employees feel supported, engagement levels increase, and productivity soars. Make it real for them—not just numbers on a slide, but a vision of what's possible.

4. Anticipate Pushback and Prepare Solutions

Innovative ideas often face resistance—whether it's fear of change, concerns about feasibility, or skepticism about results. Anticipating objections and addressing them proactively will show that you've thought through your proposal and are prepared to deliver solutions.

- **Identify Common Objections:** Think about what challenges your audience might raise—budget constraints, implementation concerns, or skepticism about outcomes.

- **Prepare Counterarguments:** Have data, examples, or alternative solutions ready to address these concerns head-on.
- **Focus on Benefits:** Reframe objections by emphasizing how the benefits outweigh the risks.

Example: Proposing a four-day workweek? Expect pushback on productivity concerns. Counter with research from companies that have successfully implemented shorter workweeks, showing increased efficiency and job satisfaction. Address concerns by suggesting a pilot program where a select team tests the model before full implementation. Show leadership that you're not just pushing for change, you're offering a thoughtful, structured approach that mitigates risk.

Practical Tips for Presenting Your Ideas

- **Know Your Audience:** Tailor your pitch to the priorities, preferences, and pain points of your audience. A finance-driven leader may need to hear about cost savings, while an HR leader might care more about employee engagement.
- **Use Visuals Strategically:** Create clear, compelling visuals (e.g., charts, infographics, or slides) to support your points and keep your audience engaged.
- **Be Concise:** Avoid overloading your pitch with details. Present your idea clearly and succinctly, leaving room for questions or discussion.

Example in Action:

Scenario: You want to introduce a flexible working arrangement in your organization.

- **Framing with Data:** Start by citing research from companies that have successfully adopted hybrid or flexible models, showing increases in productivity, employee satisfaction, and retention.

- **Alignment with Goals:** Emphasize how this aligns with the company's stated commitment to work-life balance, employee well-being, and innovation.
- **Storytelling:** Share a relatable anecdote about an employee from another company who thrived under a flexible schedule, leading to tangible business outcomes.
- **Anticipating Pushback:** Be ready to address concerns about accountability by suggesting tools like project management software or regular team check-ins to ensure productivity.

Pitch Summary:
"Flexible working arrangements have proven to increase productivity by 20% and reduce employee turnover by 15%, according to a study by XYZ Consulting. This initiative aligns with our company's value of prioritizing employee well-being while supporting innovation. Imagine the impact of having a happier, more engaged workforce that's empowered to deliver results. I propose piloting this model with one department, using tools like [specific software] to track performance and productivity. We can evaluate the results in six months to determine scalability."

Key Takeaway

Presenting unconventional ideas in traditional spaces requires a balance of creativity and strategy. By anchoring your proposals in data, aligning them with organizational goals, and delivering them with compelling storytelling, you can position yourself as an innovative leader who drives meaningful change. Push past the fear of rejection or skepticism—your unique perspective and bold ideas are exactly what corporate spaces need to evolve and thrive.

Examples of How Creativity Builds Leadership Credibility

Creativity isn't just about generating bold ideas—it's about transforming challenges into opportunities and consistently delivering innovative solutions that add value. Leaders who demonstrate creativity are often seen as more adaptable, visionary, and influential because they inspire trust in their ability to navigate uncertainty and drive meaningful change. As a Black professional, creativity can also serve as a tool to challenge stereotypes, disrupt traditional norms, and showcase unique perspectives that others might overlook.

Here are some real examples of how creativity builds leadership credibility:

Case Study 1: The Tech Innovator

A director at a leading tech company identified inefficiencies in their team's workflow that were causing delays and frustration. Instead of accepting the status quo, they proposed developing an AI-powered tool to automate repetitive tasks and improve efficiency.

Initially, the idea was met with skepticism. Some stakeholders questioned the feasibility and return on investment, while team members worried about potential job displacement. Recognizing these concerns, the director approached the challenge strategically:

- Gathered data to **quantify the time lost** to inefficiencies and demonstrated how automation could free up employees for higher-value work.
- Presented a **clear development roadmap**, outlining implementation strategies and expected outcomes.
- Engaged **cross-functional teams** to ensure buy-in and incorporated feedback at every stage.

Once launched, the tool exceeded expectations, reducing workflow time by 40% and boosting overall productivity. It became a company-wide standard, positioning the director as an innovative, solution-oriented leader whose creativity translated into measurable business impact.

Lesson: *Creativity isn't just about brainstorming bold ideas—it's also about identifying inefficiencies, leveraging existing skills, and methodically driving innovation that solves real problems.*

Case Study 2: The Strategic Thinker

A senior project manager at a consulting firm was tasked with developing a strategy for a client struggling to engage underserved communities. Traditional market research approaches had failed to yield meaningful insights, so the project manager proposed a community-driven strategy that directly involved local stakeholders.

Their approach included:

- **Hosting town halls and focus groups** to gather firsthand insights from the community.
- **Collaborating with local leaders** to co-create solutions that felt authentic and actionable.
- **Using creative storytelling techniques** to present findings in a way that resonated emotionally with the client's leadership team.

The result was a highly tailored strategy that not only strengthened the client's relationship with the community but also increased engagement and brand loyalty. The project manager's ability to integrate inclusive thinking into a traditionally rigid process gained them the trust of both the client and firm leadership, solidifying their reputation as a forward-thinking leader.

Lesson: *Creativity isn't just about generating new ideas—it's about challenging conventional approaches and finding solutions that prioritize inclusivity, connection, and impact.*

Case Study 3: The Cultural Visionary

A vice president of marketing faced the challenge of revitalizing a legacy brand struggling to resonate with younger, more diverse consumers. While traditional rebranding approaches focused on generic market trends, they proposed weaving cultural narratives into the campaign—celebrating the rich diversity of the brand's customers.

Their approach included:

- **Partnering with emerging artists and influencers** from underrepresented communities to create authentic campaign visuals and messaging.
- **Highlighting customer stories** that showcased the brand's impact across generations.
- **Using data-driven insights** to ensure the campaign remained commercially viable while staying true to its cultural roots.

The campaign was a resounding success, leading to a 25% increase in brand engagement and widespread positive media coverage. By merging creativity with cultural awareness, the vice president positioned themselves as a leader with both vision and authenticity.

Lesson: *Creativity, when paired with cultural intelligence, can elevate brands, engage communities, and strengthen leadership credibility.*

The Link Between Creativity and Credibility

Creativity is more than a skill—it's a **signal of leadership potential**. It shows that you:

- **Think Beyond the Obvious:** Leaders who consistently bring fresh perspectives and innovative solutions stand out as visionaries.
- **Take Calculated Risks:** Creativity often involves stepping outside comfort zones. When these risks pay off, they showcase your ability to make bold decisions that drive results.
- **Deliver Tangible Outcomes:** Creativity gains credibility when it's backed by results—whether it's solving a persistent problem, boosting engagement, or driving innovation.

Creativity also demonstrates **resilience and resourcefulness**, particularly in navigating spaces where traditional solutions may not address the unique challenges they face.

Actionable Takeaways for Building Leadership Credibility Through Creativity

- **Spot Opportunities for Innovation:** Look for pain points, inefficiencies, or overlooked areas where your unique perspective can offer solutions.
- **Present Solutions Strategically:** Use data, storytelling, and alignment with organizational goals to gain buy-in for unconventional ideas.
- **Collaborate Creatively:** Involve diverse voices to generate ideas that are both innovative and inclusive.

- **Celebrate Wins:** Publicly share the success of creative initiatives, not only to build your credibility but also to inspire others to think differently.

Creativity in leadership is not about having all the answers, it's about asking the right questions and being bold enough to explore uncharted territory. By consistently bringing innovative, inclusive solutions to the table, you build credibility, influence, and a leadership legacy that inspires others to see creativity as a driver of meaningful progress.

Conclusion

Innovation and creativity are not just buzzwords; they are the driving forces behind impactful leadership. When change and complexity are constant, the ability to think differently, solve problems innovatively, and deliver creative solutions is what sets influential leaders apart. Creativity holds even greater significance—it's a way to challenge stereotypes, disrupt outdated norms, and showcase the unique value your perspective brings to the table.

Harnessing creativity begins with confidence in your lived experiences. These experiences, your cultural background, personal challenges, and professional journey—are the foundation for fresh, bold ideas that others may not see. By reframing those ideas strategically, aligning them with organizational goals, and presenting them with data and storytelling, you establish yourself as a leader who is not only innovative but also credible and results driven.

This chapter was to show you how creativity isn't confined to brainstorming or "thinking outside the box"—it's about building solutions that matter. Whether it's leveraging cultural insights for impactful campaigns, creating inclusive strategies that connect with broader audiences, or driving innovation through technology, creativity is a skill that elevates your leadership credibility and amplifies your impact.

Key Takeaways:

1. Creativity is not a gift reserved for a few, it's a skill you can hone by embracing your perspective and thinking boldly.
2. Presenting unconventional ideas requires strategic framing, clear alignment with goals,

and anticipation of pushback—but the rewards far outweigh the risks.
3. Creativity strengthens your leadership brand, positioning you as a forward-thinking, adaptable, and visionary leader.

Looking Ahead:

As you continue your leadership journey, creativity will be a constant companion. However, the ability to think creatively is only one part of the equation. In the next chapter, you'll explore critical thinking and decision-making—two skills that will help you navigate uncertainty, weigh risks, and drive results with clarity and confidence.

Remember, creativity is more than a tool for problem-solving—it's a form of leadership that inspires trust, drives progress, and builds a legacy that leaves spaces better than you found them. Stay bold, stay creative, and keep challenging the norms that limit potential.

Chapter 5: Thinking Big – Critical Thinking and Decision Making

Every great leader faces moments of uncertainty, where decisions must be made with incomplete information and the stakes feel high. These moments define leadership—not because of the absence of risk, but because of the ability to navigate that risk thoughtfully and strategically.

Critical thinking and decision-making often take on an added layer of complexity. You may find yourself under additional scrutiny, balancing personal goals with systemic challenges, or navigating decisions that affect not just your career but the opportunities of those who come after you. This chapter is about equipping you with the tools to think bigger, act decisively, and move through uncertainty with confidence.

You'll explore how to:

- Evaluate situations critically, even when the full picture isn't clear.

- Balance risk and reward in a way that positions you for success while protecting your long-term vision.
- Apply critical thinking skills through real-world case studies designed to strengthen your decision-making process.

Leadership is not about always having the right answers; it's about asking the right questions, analyzing options with clarity, and making decisions that move the needle forward. Let's dive in and unlock the tools to think big, act strategically, and lead with conviction.

Learning to Make Decisions with Limited Information

Effective leadership often demands the ability to act decisively, even when faced with incomplete or ambiguous information. This is particularly true in fast-paced corporate environments, where waiting for all the details can lead to missed opportunities or loss of momentum. For many of us, decision-making can carry additional weight as you navigate a particular set of expectations, potential scrutiny, and the desire to set a positive precedent for those who come after you.

The key to thriving in these high-stakes situations isn't about having all the answers, it's about developing the confidence, clarity, and flexibility to make informed choices in the face of uncertainty.

Key Points for Effective Decision-Making

1. Trust Your Expertise (In the simplest terms you know things)

Your experiences, cultural insights, and professional journey equip you with a unique and powerful decision-making lens. Often, you may hesitate to trust your intuition because of the conditioning to "prove yourself" with data or external validation. However, intuition grounded in experience is a critical leadership tool.

- **Why It Matters:** Your background has likely taught you how to navigate complex, multi-layered situations. Whether it's managing resources under constraints or reading between the lines in ambiguous communication, your intuition reflects a wealth of hard-earned wisdom.
- **How to Apply:** When faced with limited information, draw on your past successes and lessons learned. Ask yourself: *What has worked in similar situations before? What does my instinct tell me, and why?*

2. Prioritize Key Information

Not all information carries the same weight. Effective decision-making requires the ability to sift through the noise and focus on the details that directly impact the decision at hand.

- **Why It Matters:** Overanalyzing every piece of data can lead to "analysis paralysis," where the fear of missing something important delays action. By prioritizing what matters most, you can act swiftly and decisively.
- **How to Apply:** Ask yourself:
    - *What are the key outcomes I'm trying to achieve?*
    - *Which data points directly influence these outcomes?*
    - *What information can I ignore or revisit later?*

3. Scenario Planning: Prepare for Multiple Outcomes

Scenario planning is a powerful tool for decision-making under uncertainty. By envisioning potential outcomes—best, base, and worst case, you can make choices that are proactive rather than reactive.

- **Why It Matters:** Anticipating different scenarios helps you prepare for challenges, mitigate risks, and identify opportunities you might not have seen otherwise. It also builds confidence that you've considered all angles, reducing the fear of the unknown.
- **How to Apply:** When making a decision, map out the following:
    - *Best-Case Scenario:* What's the most favorable outcome, and how can you maximize it?
    - *Worst-Case Scenario:* What's the biggest risk, and how can you minimize its impact?
    - *Base Case Scenario:* Based on available information, what outcome is most realistic, and how can you prepare?

Example: A senior leader is tasked with implementing a new company-wide software system to improve productivity. However, there's uncertainty about adoption rates and potential resistance from employees. Using scenario planning, they map out:

- **Best Case**: Employees quickly adapt, efficiency improves, and the company sees measurable gains in productivity. To maximize this, the leader plans an engaging training rollout and incentives for early adoption.

- **Worst Case**: Employees resist the change, leading to a drop in productivity and frustration. To mitigate this, the leader builds in extra support resources, creates a phased implementation plan, and secures leadership buy-in to reinforce the benefits.
- **Most Likely Case**: Adoption happens gradually, with some initial pushback but steady improvements over time. To manage this, the leader prepares to track adoption trends, adjust strategies as needed, and celebrate small wins along the way.

By thinking through all possibilities, the leader positions themselves to respond strategically rather than react emotionally, ensuring the transition is as smooth as possible.

Practical Tips for Decision-Making in Ambiguity

1. **Set a Deadline for Action:** Ambiguity can tempt you to delay decisions indefinitely. Establish a clear timeline to gather information and make your call.
2. **Leverage Your Network:** Seek input from trusted colleagues or mentors who can provide additional perspectives, but don't rely on consensus to avoid accountability.
3. **Communicate Your Rationale:** When sharing your decision, explain the key factors you considered. This builds trust and credibility, even if the outcome isn't perfect.
4. **Be Willing to Pivot:** A decision made with limited information may require adjustment as new details emerge. Stay open to revisiting and refining your approach.

Example in Action

Scenario: A senior leader is tasked with restructuring a team amid budget cuts, but they have limited clarity on future staffing needs.

How to Approach:
- **Trust Your Expertise:** Reflect on past restructures or team realignments. What strategies worked? What challenges arose? Use those insights to guide initial decisions.
- **Prioritize Information:** Focus on the core business objectives, what roles are essential to maintain operations, and where can efficiencies be created?
- **Scenario Planning:** Anticipate potential shifts. If additional funding becomes available, how would you scale back up? If deeper cuts are required, what's the contingency plan?

By making a well-reasoned decision while allowing room for adjustments, the leader demonstrates confidence, clarity, and agility—qualities that define strong leadership in uncertain times.

Making decisions with limited information is a hallmark of effective leadership because it requires clarity, confidence, and courage. It's also a way to challenge narratives that question your judgment or readiness for high-stakes roles. Every decision you make with conviction reinforces your credibility and positions you as a leader capable of navigating complexity.

Leadership isn't about always knowing the perfect answer, it's about making the best possible choice with what you have and adjusting as you learn more. By mastering this skill, you unlock the ability to think big, act decisively, and lead with impact, even when the path ahead is uncertain.

Balancing Risk and Reward in Leadership

Risk-taking is an integral part of leadership, but it's not just about being bold for the sake of it—it's about making calculated decisions that will bring a significant return. Balancing risk and reward requires assessing potential outcomes, understanding your tolerance for risk, and knowing how to mitigate potential downsides.

Steps to Balance Risk and Reward:

1. **Assess Potential Impact:** What are the potential benefits if the decision pays off? What are the repercussions if it fails? Evaluate these factors to determine whether the potential rewards justify the risks.

2. **Seek Diverse Perspectives:** Solicit feedback from people with different viewpoints and experiences to get a well-rounded understanding of potential risks and outcomes.

3. **Prepare Contingency Plans:** Have "Plan B" strategies in place to reduce potential fallout should things not go as planned.

Example: Leadership often requires stepping into uncertainty and making decisions that can redefine the course of a team or organization.

When I stepped into a program management leadership role, I quickly realized there was no documentation, no established processes, and no clear procedures in place. The lack of structure made it difficult to run the program efficiently, and I knew that without foundational systems, productivity and engagement would suffer. Instead of waiting for direction or risking burnout by trying to manage chaos, I took the initiative to build what was missing.

I created processes, documented best practices, and implemented procedures to streamline operations. The result? Engagement increased, productivity improved, and the program became more sustainable for both me and future leaders. What started as a challenge became an opportunity to transform the way the team functioned.

Similarly, consider a leader at a mid-sized company who proposed a significant investment in an untested technology to streamline operations. While it had the potential to greatly improve productivity, it also came with financial risk. Instead of diving in blindly, the leader consulted with their team, researched similar case studies, and designed a phased implementation plan. By proposing a pilot phase, they minimized risk while testing the technology's impact. The pilot yielded promising results, allowing the company to invest with greater confidence.

Risk in leadership isn't about recklessness—it's about strategic decision-making. Whether implementing new processes, investing in technology, or restructuring a team, great leaders recognize that thoughtful planning and calculated risks lead to lasting impact.

Exercises: Create Your Own Case Studies for Honing Critical Thinking Skills

Exercise 1: The "What-If" Scenario Drill

Choose a decision you've faced in the past where you had limited information. Take 15 minutes to outline three different scenarios: the best outcome, the worst outcome, and a "middle ground" outcome. Write down how you would have adjusted your approach based on these outcomes.

Exercise 2: Risk Assessment Matrix

Use a simple risk assessment matrix to evaluate an upcoming decision. List potential actions along one axis and potential risks along the other. Rate each risk by likelihood and impact, then determine which actions align with your risk tolerance and objectives.

Exercise 3: The Peer Review Pitch

Present a decision you're contemplating to a peer or mentor who has a different perspective. Ask them to play "devil's advocate" and challenge your assumptions. This exercise helps identify potential weaknesses and ensures you've considered a range of perspectives.

Example Case Study:

You're considering whether to take on a high-profile project that has been offered to your team. The project promises visibility but demands a high commitment of resources. Use the risk assessment matrix to consider the project's pros and cons, potential client feedback, and your team's current capacity.

Conclusion

Thinking big isn't just about dreaming; it's about applying critical thinking and decision-making skills that can move your career and your organization forward. In this chapter we explored the essentials of making decisions with limited information, balancing risk and reward, and honing these skills through practical exercises.

Next, we'll shift to amplifying your leadership voice and building influence in ways that reflect your unique strengths and perspectives.

Chapter 6: Building Bridges – Collaboration and Influence

The Art of Building Allies Across Departments and Levels

Collaboration is essential for career growth and organizational success, yet it's not always intuitive, especially when working across different teams and hierarchies. To advance your career and make impactful change, building strong allies and coalitions is crucial. These alliances can provide support, offer new perspectives, and help you amplify your voice in decision-making spaces.

Key Points for Building Allies:
- **Identify Shared Goals:** To build allies, identify common objectives that can lead to mutually beneficial outcomes. Collaborating on shared projects or initiatives is a natural way to establish a bond.
- **Communicate with Transparency:** Be open about your goals and intentions. Transparency helps build trust and encourages others to work with you.

- **Be Generous with Support:** Offer help and show genuine interest in others' work. Helping colleagues, even without immediate personal gain, creates goodwill and encourages reciprocity.

Example: Picture that you are leading a high-priority project that requires input from multiple departments. Some colleagues may be hesitant to collaborate, fearing competing priorities or additional workload. Instead of working in isolation, you proactively set up regular check-ins with key stakeholders, ensuring that their perspectives are valued. You listen to their concerns, adjust strategies when necessary, and contribute thoughtful ideas that align with shared goals. Over time, this builds trust and credibility, positioning you as a bridge-builder who can facilitate communication and problem-solving across teams.

Strategies to Lead Teams with Diverse Personalities and Perspectives

Leading a team composed of individuals with varied backgrounds, personalities, and perspectives can be both rewarding and challenging. To foster collaboration and guide your team effectively, you need to leverage their differences to create a stronger, more innovative group.

Key Strategies for Leading Diverse Teams:

1. **Develop Empathetic Leadership Skills:** Empathy is a cornerstone of effective leadership. Understanding your team members' unique motivations and challenges allows you to lead in a way that supports them and maximizes their contributions.

2. **Adapt Your Communication Style:** Different team members may respond better to different communication methods, some may prefer direct, task-oriented discussions, while others thrive with more collaborative and conversational approaches.

3. **Encourage Inclusivity in Decision-Making:** Create opportunities for team members to voice their opinions and contribute to decisions. This approach can boost team morale and foster a sense of ownership and inclusion.

Example: You are leading a newly formed cross-functional team, and you notice that one of your team members, who is introverted, has valuable insights but feels overshadowed during discussions. Instead of letting their contributions go unheard, you implement structured one-on-one check-ins where they can confidently share their input. Additionally, you rotate facilitation roles in meetings, giving different team members the opportunity to lead discussions. As a result, the team benefits from diverse viewpoints, and the individual feels more empowered to participate in larger conversations.

Tips for Navigating Difficult Team Dynamics While Maintaining Harmony

Difficult team dynamics can challenge your leadership and influence. When conflicts arise, whether due to miscommunication, competing agendas, or contrasting opinions, maintaining harmony while ensuring that productivity isn't sacrificed is crucial.

Tips for Managing Difficult Dynamics:

- **Establish Clear Boundaries and Expectations:** Set clear ground rules for communication and behavior at the start of any project or meeting. These guidelines create a structured environment that minimizes misunderstandings and disputes.
- **Leverage Conflict as an Opportunity for Growth:** Use conflict to identify areas for improvement within the team and find solutions that can enhance collaboration. Approach disagreements as opportunities for constructive dialogue.
- **Act as a Mediator:** Be prepared to step in and act as an impartial mediator when conflicts become counterproductive. Facilitating open and respectful conversations can help bring resolution and unity.

Example: Imagine leading a team where two members frequently clash due to their different working styles. One is highly detail-oriented and prefers structured processes, while the other is a big-picture thinker who values flexibility and innovation. Recognizing the tension, you hold a structured alignment meeting, where both individuals outline their priorities and concerns. You then clarify roles and responsibilities that leverage their strengths—allowing the detail-oriented colleague to focus on execution while the strategic thinker leads brainstorming initiatives. By setting clear expectations and fostering collaboration, you turn a potential conflict into a productive working relationship.

Building bridges and leading diverse teams are essential for long-term success in corporate environments. By proactively forming alliances, recognizing the strengths of different personalities, and effectively managing conflict, you set the stage for stronger collaboration and influence.

Exercises to Strengthening Your Collaborative Skills

Exercise 1: The Cross-Departmental Coffee Chat

One of the best ways to strengthen collaboration is by proactively building relationships with colleagues outside of your immediate team. This helps break down silos, fosters new ideas, and expands your influence within the organization.

Step 1: Identify a Colleague to Connect With

Think about someone from another department whose work you admire or who works on projects that interest you. This could be someone in marketing, HR, finance, IT, or another function that intersects with your own.

Step 2: Reach Out to Set Up the Meeting

Here's an example email or message you could send: *"Hi [Name], I've been following your work on [specific project or initiative], and I'd love to learn more about your role and the challenges your team is working on. If you're open to it, I'd love to grab a quick coffee or set up a 20-minute virtual chat to exchange insights. Let me know if you'd be available sometime this week or next!"*

Step 3: Conduct the Chat

During the conversation, ask open-ended questions like:

- *What are the biggest priorities for your team right now?*
- *What challenges do you face in your role?*
- *How do you see our teams working together more effectively?*

Step 4: Capture Insights and Apply Them

After the meeting, write down key takeaways. Did you learn something that could improve your own work? Are there opportunities for collaboration? Follow up with a quick thank-you note and mention any ideas sparked from your discussion.

You've built a new connection, gained insight into another part of the business, and laid the groundwork for future collaboration.

Exercise 2: Empathy Mapping

Empathy is key to understanding different perspectives and improving team dynamics. This exercise helps you analyze a colleague's motivations, challenges, and perspectives to improve communication and collaboration.

Step 1: Choose a Colleague with a Different Perspective

Pick someone you sometimes struggle to understand, perhaps they have a different work style, communication approach, or priorities than you do.

Step 2: Create an Empathy Map

Divide a page into four quadrants labeled:
Says – What do they verbally express about their work, challenges, or priorities?
Thinks – What might they be thinking but not saying? What are their unspoken concerns?
Feels – What emotions might be driving their actions (stress, excitement, frustration)?
Does – How do they behave in meetings, emails, or projects?

Example Empathy Map for a Detail-Oriented Colleague:

Says	Thinks
"I need more data before we move forward."	"If we rush this, mistakes will happen."
"Let's stick to the process."	"Why doesn't everyone follow the same structure?"
Feels	**Does**
Stressed by last-minute changes	Double-checks all work before sharing
Frustrated when decisions feel rushed	Prefers clear guidelines and structured plans

Step 3: Use Insights to Improve Collaboration

Now that you see their perspective, adjust your approach. If they value structure, provide clear agendas and expectations ahead of time. If they're risk-averse, present data to support decisions.

This exercise helps you anticipate concerns, adapt communication styles, and foster stronger working relationships.

Exercise 3: The Conflict Resolution Role-Play

Difficult conversations are part of leadership. Practicing how to mediate disagreements and communicate effectively can help you resolve conflicts with confidence.

Step 1: Identify a Trusted Partner

Find a colleague, mentor, or peer who can help you role-play a difficult conversation. Here's how to ask:

Example Message:

"Hey [Name], I'm working on improving my conflict resolution skills and was wondering if you'd be open to a quick role-play exercise with me. I'd love to practice handling [a disagreement, tough feedback, etc.] and get your perspective. Let me know if you'd be up for it!"

Step 2: Role-Play the Conversation

Choose a real or hypothetical scenario. Common conflicts include:

- A colleague not pulling their weight on a project
- A team member resisting feedback or change
- A disagreement over priorities or deadlines

Practice both sides of the conversation—first as yourself, then as the other person. Focus on:

- Active listening (*"I hear that you're frustrated about..."*)
- Paraphrasing to clarify (*"So what I'm hearing is..."*)
- Staying neutral and solution-focused (*"How can we meet in the middle?"*)

Step 3: Reflect and Adjust

After the role-play, ask for feedback:

- *Did I come across as open and solution-oriented?*

- *What could I have done differently?*
- *How would you have approached this situation?*

By practicing in a low stakes setting, you'll feel more prepared to handle real conflicts calmly and effectively.

Conclusion

Building strong relationships, understanding different perspectives, and managing conflict are all essential leadership skills. Collaboration isn't just about working with others, it's about fostering an environment where everyone feels valued and heard.

Next Steps:

✓ **Schedule a cross-departmental coffee chat** this month.

✓ **Pick a team member and create an empathy map** to better understand their perspective.

✓ **Practice a difficult conversation with a trusted colleague** to strengthen your conflict resolution skills.

By making collaboration a daily habit, you'll increase your influence, strengthen your leadership, and create a workplace where diverse voices thrive.

Next, we'll explore how your personal and professional creativity can set you apart as an influential leader.

Chapter 7: Owning the Room – Communication for Impact

Crafting Your Message for Clarity and Persuasion

Effective communication is at the heart of influential leadership. Whether you are pitching an idea in a board meeting, advocating for a new initiative, or leading a team, the way you communicate can make or break your impact. Crafting messages that are clear, concise, and persuasive is a skill that sets great leaders apart.

Key Points for Crafting Your Message:
- **Know Your Audience:** Tailor your message to resonate with the interests and needs of your listeners. Understand their background, goals, and values to create content that engages and persuades.
- **Use the Power of Structure:** Start with a strong opening that captures attention, follow with main points supported by evidence or examples, and end with a memorable conclusion and CTA (call to action). This classic approach ensures that your audience remains engaged from start to finish.

- **Be Authentic and Confident:** Authenticity builds trust. Speak with conviction and ensure your message aligns with your core values and beliefs. Confidence can be the differentiator between being heard or being overlooked.

Example: Picture that you are proposing a new initiative to senior leadership. Rather than jumping into technical details, you start with a compelling problem statement—something that immediately captures attention. You follow with key data points that highlight the significance of the issue, making your case undeniable. As you present your proposal, you weave in a real-world example of a competitor who successfully implemented a similar initiative, proving its viability. Finally, you close with a clear call to action, outlining next steps and reinforcing your commitment to leading the effort. By structuring your message this way, you ensure it is engaging, evidence-based, and action-driven—exactly what decision-makers need to hear.

Public Speaking and Storytelling as Leadership Tools

Public speaking and storytelling are more than just techniques for making speeches; they are powerful leadership tools that allow you to inspire, connect, and persuade. Using stories effectively can humanize your message, making it relatable and memorable.

Key Strategies for Effective Public Speaking and Storytelling:

- **Connect Emotionally:** People remember stories that evoke emotions. Share experiences that resonate with your audience and illustrate your points. This connection can make you more relatable and trustworthy as a leader.
- **Structure Your Story:** Use a narrative arc that includes a beginning (the setup), middle (the challenge), and end (the resolution). This makes your story engaging and easy to follow.
- **Practice Active Engagement:** Use pauses, variations in tone, and eye contact to keep your audience engaged. Encourage questions or reactions to maintain an interactive dynamic.

Example: You are leading a quarterly team meeting, introducing a major strategic shift. Instead of immediately presenting slides filled with data, you begin with a story—a time when you personally faced a similar challenge and overcame it. You describe the obstacles, the tough decisions, and the eventual breakthrough, making it clear that change is difficult, but possible. Then, you transition into the new strategy, explaining how it aligns with past lessons and why it will lead to success. Your team is far more receptive to the change, because they can see themselves in the story and trust your leadership through uncertainty.

Handling Tough Conversations with Poise

Navigating difficult conversations is a vital skill for leaders who want to maintain trust, inspire respect, and foster a positive environment. Whether addressing performance issues, providing constructive feedback, or discussing sensitive topics, your ability to handle these conversations with poise will set the tone for how you're perceived as a leader.

Tips for Managing Tough Conversations:

- **Prepare Ahead of Time:** Plan your key points, anticipate potential responses, and prepare how you will handle them. This helps you stay composed and focused during the conversation.
- **Stay Calm and Centered:** Practice techniques to manage your emotions, such as deep breathing or positive affirmations, before and during the conversation. A calm demeanor can prevent escalation and help maintain a productive atmosphere.
- **Use Active Listening and Empathy:** Listen more than you speak and show that you understand the other person's perspective. Validate their feelings and then guide the conversation toward a solution-focused dialogue.
- **Be Solution-Oriented:** Frame the conversation with a goal of finding common ground and fostering improvement. Make sure to follow up with actionable steps and support.

Example: Suppose you need to discuss an underperforming team member's work. Instead of starting with criticism, you set a supportive tone, acknowledging their past contributions. Then, you bring up the specific challenges, using concrete examples rather than vague feedback. You ask open-ended questions, giving them space to share their perspective. As the conversation unfolds, you collaborate on a realistic improvement plan, ensuring they have the support needed to succeed. While resolution may not happen immediately, you leave the discussion with mutual understanding and a clear path forward.

Great leaders are great communicators. Whether you're persuading decision-makers, inspiring a team, or handling tough conversations, your ability to craft clear messages, tell compelling stories, and navigate challenges with poise will define your leadership presence.

By mastering communication, you own the room, amplify your influence, and drive meaningful change in any setting.

Exercises: Enhancing Your Communication Skills

These exercises will help you sharpen your communication, build confidence, and refine your ability to influence others. Strong communicators own the room, whether in one-on-one conversations, team meetings, or high-stakes presentations.

Exercise 1: Craft Your Elevator Pitch

An elevator pitch is a concise, compelling summary of who you are, what you do, and what makes you stand out. It should be clear, engaging, and memorable, something you could confidently deliver in under 30 seconds to a senior executive, potential mentor, or networking contact.

Step 1: Structure Your Pitch

Use this framework:

1. **Who You Are:** Your role and expertise
2. **What You Do:** The value you bring or problems you solve
3. **Why It Matters:** What makes you unique or the impact of your work
4. **Call to Action:** An invitation to continue the conversation

Example: *"I lead diversity-focused leadership programs that help organizations retain and advance underrepresented talent. My work has increased leadership representation by 30% in the past two years. I'm passionate about creating workplaces where diverse talent thrives—let's connect on ways to scale that impact."*

Step 2: Practice for Confidence

- **Deliver it in front of a mirror** to work on tone, pacing, and expression.

- **Record yourself** and listen for areas to refine.
- **Try it with a colleague** and ask for feedback, does it sound clear and engaging?

A polished, natural-sounding pitch that makes an immediate impact in any professional setting.

Exercise 2: Storytelling for Impact

Storytelling is a powerful leadership tool that makes your message memorable, relatable, and persuasive. Whether presenting an idea or motivating your team, storytelling draws people in and connects them emotionally to your message.

Step 1: Choose a Leadership Story

Think of a real experience that taught you an important lesson about leadership, resilience, or innovation. A strong story follows this three-part structure:

1. **The Setup:** Describe the challenge or situation.
2. **The Struggle:** Explain the obstacles, setbacks, or tough decisions.
3. **The Solution & Lesson:** Share how the challenge was overcome and what you learned.

Example: Picture leading a high-stakes project that was on the brink of failure. You had to rally a demotivated team, pivot the strategy, and regain leadership's confidence. Through communication and persistence, the project turned around, leading to a major win for the company.

Step 2: Practice with Emotion & Delivery

- **Write it out first** to refine key points.
- **Tell it aloud** while emphasizing emotion—people connect with feelings, not just facts.
- **Test it with a peer** and ask:
    - *Did it feel authentic?*

- Was the lesson clear?
- What could make it more compelling?

A strong leadership story you can use in presentations, team meetings, or networking conversations to engage and inspire others.

Exercise 3: Role-Playing Tough Conversations

Difficult conversations are unavoidable in leadership, whether addressing underperformance, managing conflict, or giving tough feedback. Practicing them in a low-risk setting will make real-life situations feel more manageable.

Step 1: Choose a Realistic Scenario

Pick a situation you might face, such as:
- A team member missing deadlines consistently
- A colleague taking credit for your work
- A disagreement over priorities with another department

Step 2: Find a Trusted Partner

Ask a mentor, peer, or friend:

Example Message:

"I'm working on improving my ability to navigate tough conversations and would love to practice with you. Could we do a quick role-play where I address [specific issue]? Your feedback would be really valuable!"

Step 3: Role-Play the Conversation

- Take turns playing both roles—the leader and the recipient.
- Focus on active listening, keeping the tone professional, and steering the discussion toward solutions.

- If emotions run high, practice pausing and re-centering before responding.

A higher level of comfort and preparedness for handling tough conversations with confidence and clarity.

These exercises will help you develop a strong presence, deliver messages with clarity, and navigate difficult discussions with poise.

Conclusion

Communication is an indispensable part of effective leadership. From crafting messages that resonate to mastering public speaking and navigating tough conversations, communication shapes how others perceive you and how successfully you lead. This chapter has provided practical tools and examples to help you communicate with impact.

Up next, we'll explore how to harness your creativity and strategic thinking to further enhance your leadership capabilities.

Chapter 8: Setting Your Sights on the C-Suite

Creating a Vision for Your Career

Success in reaching the C-suite requires more than just hard work and a strong track record. It requires clarity, intention, and a clear vision. A vision provides the roadmap that guides your decisions, prioritizes your efforts, and positions you strategically for leadership opportunities.

Key Points for Creating a Vision:

- **Identify Your Long-Term Aspirations:** Reflect on what you want to achieve in your career and why. Is it to lead an entire department, influence industry standards, or innovate within your company? Understand the 'why' behind your goal to give it deeper meaning.
- **Visualize Your Ideal Position:** Picture yourself in the role you want to attain. How does it align with your strengths, interests, and values? Take note of the attributes and achievements that got you there.
- **Align Vision with Personal Values:** Ensure that your vision supports your personal beliefs and values. This alignment will make your journey more fulfilling and sustainable, helping

you navigate challenges while staying true to yourself.

Example: If your goal is to become Chief Operating Officer (COO), envision what it would look like to hold that position, including what you'd be doing daily, how you'd be influencing company culture, and the legacy you'd leave. Your vision isn't just about securing the title, it's about driving operational excellence, improving efficiency, and ensuring seamless execution of business strategies. In this role, you would be overseeing company-wide processes, aligning business functions, and optimizing workflows to scale the company's success. You would be the bridge between vision and execution, ensuring that strategic initiatives are not only well-planned but also effectively implemented.

With this clear vision in mind, every opportunity—from the projects you take on to the mentors you seek—should bring you closer to that reality.

SMART Goal Setting Tailored to Your Professional Journey

Having a vision is essential, but translating it into **actionable, measurable steps** is what moves your career forward. SMART (Specific, Measurable, Achievable, Relevant, Time-bound) goals provide **structure** that ensures your progress is both **visible and strategic**—especially when working toward **gaining positive visibility as an operational leader**.

Picture that you want to establish yourself as a leader in process improvement and operational efficiency within your company. Instead of setting a vague goal like "improve my leadership presence," break it down into a SMART framework:

Goal: Lead a company-wide initiative that improves operational efficiency and secures executive recognition within the next six months.

- **Specific:** Identify an inefficiency in the company's supply chain or internal processes, develop a solution, and lead an initiative to implement improvements.
- **Measurable:** Reduce operational costs by **10%**, cut down project turnaround time by **20%**, or improve team efficiency based on internal KPIs.
- **Achievable:** Leverage existing cross-functional relationships, gather insights from key departments, and collaborate with internal teams to implement changes.
- **Relevant:** Aligns with the COO role's core responsibilities—process optimization, cost reduction, and operational scalability.

- **Time-bound:** Identify the area for improvement within one month, implement changes within three months, and measure impact by month six.

By breaking your goal into measurable actions, you ensure that your visibility isn't just accidental—it's intentional, recognized, and tied to executive leadership readiness.

Exercises: Writing Your Leadership Development Plan

A leadership development plan provides a structured approach to career growth, ensuring that you are actively working toward the skills, experiences, and relationships necessary to secure senior leadership roles. Whether you are striving for a Senior Director role or aiming for the COO position, having a plan allows you to make strategic, intentional moves that align with your long-term vision.

Below are two distinct Leadership Development Plan Structures—one for a Senior Director and another for a COO position.

Exercise 1: Identify Key Career Milestones

List major positions and achievements that will propel you to executive leadership. These milestones should reflect increasing responsibility, strategic impact, and visibility. Examples may include:

- Leading enterprise-wide initiatives that drive measurable business outcomes.
- Managing P&L responsibilities to gain financial oversight experience.
- Driving cross-functional collaboration between departments to improve efficiency and effectiveness.
- Securing a seat at executive-level strategy discussions by leading major operational transformations.
- Being recognized externally through industry speaking engagements, advisory boards, or executive panels.

By outlining these milestones, you clarify what key steps must be taken to move to the next level.

Exercise 2: Mapping Out Skill Gaps

Identify leadership skills or competencies that are critical for executive success but may require further development.

- **Strategic Decision-Making:** Enhance your ability to make high-stakes decisions that impact business direction.
    - **Action Plan:** Shadow senior executives, participate in corporate strategy meetings, and take executive leadership courses.
- **Financial Acumen:** Deepen your understanding of budgeting, forecasting, and profit/loss management.
    - **Action Plan:** Take a finance for non-financial executives' course, oversee departmental budgets, or engage with the finance team.
- **Executive Presence & Influence:** Strengthen communication and persuasion skills to gain stakeholder buy-in at the highest levels.
    - **Action Plan:** Present at executive meetings, seek media training, and engage in high-visibility leadership forums.

By proactively closing these gaps, you ensure that you're prepared for leadership responsibilities when opportunities arise.

Exercise 3: Building Your Support Network

Identify the key people who can advocate for your leadership growth:

- **Mentors** – Senior executives who can provide guidance, advice, and leadership insights.
- **Sponsors** – Leaders who actively advocate for your promotions and leadership visibility.
- **Peers** – Trusted colleagues who serve as sounding boards and collaborators for strategic initiatives.

Actionable Step: Within the next month, reach out to a mentor or sponsor to discuss career development opportunities and gain insight into executive leadership expectations.

Example Leadership Development Plan Structure:

Leadership Development Plan for a Senior Director Position

1. Vision Statement

"To transition from Senior Director to Vice President by demonstrating strategic leadership, driving operational excellence, and influencing key business decisions."

2. SMART Goals

Lead a critical business initiative within the next 12 months

- Specific: Identify and execute an initiative that improves efficiency, cost savings, or scalability.
- Measurable: Deliver a **10-15% improvement** in operational KPIs.
- Achievable: Work with senior leaders to align the initiative with corporate goals.
- Relevant: Positions you as a leader with enterprise-wide impact.
- Time-bound: Initiative launched in **3 months**; results measured in **12 months**.

Gain experience managing P&L responsibilities within 18 months

- Specific: Oversee a **$5M+ budget** within your department.
- Measurable: Achieve budget accuracy within **5% of forecasts**.
- Achievable: Partner with finance and request oversight of cost centers.
- Relevant: Direct financial oversight is critical for VP and C-suite roles.

- Time-bound: Full P&L responsibility **within 18 months**.

3. Skill Development Plan
- Enroll in **executive leadership training** focused on operations, finance, and innovation.
- Increase **visibility with senior leadership** through executive presentations.
- Strengthen **influence and negotiation skills** through strategic stakeholder engagements.

4. Timeline & Checkpoints
- **Quarter 1:** Identify and propose a business-critical initiative.
- **Quarter 2-3:** Execute and measure progress.
- **Quarter 4:** Present results and seek additional leadership responsibilities.

5. Support & Accountability
- **Mentor/Sponsor:** Executive VP or COO.
- **Peer Network:** Cross-functional directors leading similar initiatives.
- **Quarterly Review:** Track progress and adjust the plan as needed.

Conclusion

Reaching senior leadership and the C-suite isn't about waiting for opportunities, it's about strategically positioning yourself for them. A clear vision, structured goal setting, and an intentional leadership development plan will ensure that every step you take moves you closer to your career aspirations.

The path to the C-suite is demanding, but it's also an opportunity to shape business strategy, drive meaningful change, and leave a lasting impact. As you move forward, your ability to balance ambition with resilience will be just as important as your leadership skills.

Next, we'll explore how to sustain your momentum by maintaining balance, protecting your well-being, and navigating challenges with resilience—so you can thrive at the top, not just survive.

Chapter 9: Self-Advocacy Without Apology

Asking for What You Want—and Getting It

Self-advocacy is a non-negotiable skill for career growth, especially as a Black professional navigating corporate spaces where our contributions may not always be automatically recognized. The ability to articulate your value and advocate for yourself—whether for a promotion, raise, or leadership opportunity—is what ensures you don't just do great work, but that you're rewarded for it.

Steps for Effective Self-Advocacy:

1. **Prepare with Evidence:** When advocating for yourself, have data or specific examples of your accomplishments. This could be quantitative results from a project you led, feedback from peers or supervisors, or any recognition you've received.
2. **Choose the Right Time and Place:** Be strategic about when and how you advocate for yourself. Timing your conversation when decision-makers are more receptive (e.g., during performance reviews or project debriefs) can yield better results.

3. **Use Confident Language:** Practice using language that clearly communicates your contributions and ambitions without apologies. Phrases like "I am proud of the outcome of [project] because it contributed to [results]" demonstrate confidence.
4. **Position Yourself as an Asset:** Frame your "ask" in terms of **business value**—how your promotion or raise will **benefit the company** rather than just focusing on personal gain.

Example: You're seeking a promotion to Senior Manager. Instead of vaguely stating that you "deserve it," you prepare a structured case:

"Over the past year, I led a process optimization project that reduced turnaround time by 30%, saving the company $500K. I also mentored two junior colleagues who were later promoted, strengthening our leadership pipeline. Given my impact on efficiency and team development, I'd like to discuss my path to Senior Manager and how I can continue driving results at the next level."

By presenting clear outcomes, you eliminate ambiguity and reinforce your leadership value.

How to Highlight Your Achievements While Remaining a Team Player

Self-promotion can feel uncomfortable, particularly when navigating stereotypes about assertiveness. However, visibility doesn't have to come at the expense of humility. The key is to highlight both your leadership and the collective success of your team.

Strategies for Highlighting Achievements:

1. **Frame Success in a Team Context:** Instead of "I achieved X," say "I led a team that accomplished X." This reinforces collaboration while making your leadership clear.

2. **Use the "Impact Statement" Approach:** Instead of simply listing achievements, explain the broader impact of your work. For example, instead of saying, "I led a team of 10 and achieved X," frame it as, "Leading a team of 10, we achieved X, which increased department efficiency by 15%."

3. **Leverage Stories and Examples:** People resonate with stories more than with statistics alone. Use anecdotes that capture your problem-solving and leadership abilities to make your achievements more relatable.

Example: Updating your LinkedIn profile or resume to highlight a major achievement:
"Spearheaded a cross-functional initiative to revamp the onboarding process, improving new hire retention by 40% and reducing training costs by $200K. This initiative streamlined workflows across three departments and increased overall employee engagement."

This approach frames your success in a way that highlights leadership, collaboration, and measurable results.

Building a Personal Brand That Speaks for Itself

A strong personal brand isn't just a tool for career growth; it's a testament to your expertise and leadership presence. Your brand should communicate who you are, what you stand for, and why you're a valuable asset to any organization.

Steps for Building a Personal Brand:

1. **Define Your Core Message:** Clearly communicate your unique strengths and values. For example, if you're known for your innovation and collaborative approach, highlight these qualities in your profiles and interactions.
   - What are the three key themes that define your expertise? (e.g., Operational Excellence, Inclusive Leadership, Strategic Growth).
   - What problem do you solve? (e.g., I help organizations scale efficiently by streamlining processes and optimizing team performance.).
2. **Consistency Across Platforms:** Make sure your personal brand is reflected across your resume, LinkedIn profile, social media, and any public-facing materials. Consistency builds trust and recognition.
   - Update your LinkedIn profile, company bio, and resume to reflect your leadership narrative.

- Engage in industry discussions, comment on relevant posts, and share insights that align with your expertise.

3. **Active Networking:** Engage with peers, mentors, and leaders who resonate with your brand. Consistently seek opportunities to share your knowledge, contribute to discussions, and showcase your skills.
    - Write **articles, blog posts, or LinkedIn content** about topics relevant to your field.
    - Speak on panels, lead internal company discussions, or host webinars.

4. **Authenticity and Vulnerability:** Being genuine and transparent about your experiences, including challenges you've faced, allows others to connect with you on a deeper level. This can make your brand more relatable and impactful.
    - Share success stories but make them value-driven—focusing on impact rather than just accomplishments.

***Example*:** If your personal brand is about operational efficiency and innovation, your LinkedIn profile might feature:

"I'm passionate about creating scalable, high-performing teams by optimizing workflows and fostering inclusive leadership. Through process innovation, I've helped organizations reduce operational inefficiencies by 30%, leading to increased profitability and employee engagement."

By defining what you stand for, engaging with your network, and demonstrating consistent leadership presence, your brand becomes your strongest career asset.

Conclusion

Self-advocacy is not just about speaking up for yourself, it's about ensuring that your work, expertise, and leadership are recognized and valued.

By mastering the ability to:

- **Confidently ask for what you want**—whether it's a raise, promotion, or leadership opportunity.
- **Highlight your achievements strategically**—balancing self-promotion with team collaboration.
- **Build a personal brand that commands respect and visibility**—ensuring that your leadership presence speaks for itself.

You position yourself for long-term success, influence, and career advancement—without apology.

Next, we'll explore how to sustain your momentum by maintaining resilience, protecting your well-being, and navigating challenges with confidence—so you can thrive at every stage of your career

Chapter 10: Mentorship and Sponsorship

The Difference Between Mentors and Sponsors—and Why You Need Both

Understanding the distinction between mentors and sponsors is crucial for advancing in your career. Both relationships offer significant benefits, but they serve different purposes.

Mentorship vs. Sponsorship

- **Mentor:** A mentor is someone who provides guidance, shares their knowledge, offers advice, and helps you develop your skills. Mentors can be an invaluable source of wisdom, helping you navigate challenges and grow professionally.
- **Sponsor:** A sponsor, on the other hand, is someone who actively advocates for you behind closed doors. They use their influence to champion your skills and put your name forward for promotions, opportunities, and key projects. Sponsors don't just offer advice; they create opportunities for you by leveraging their own reputation and connections.

Why You Need Both:

Mentors provide the knowledge and support that help you build a solid foundation for your career, while sponsors take that foundation and propel you forward into roles that showcase your abilities. Mentorship helps you build confidence and skill, while sponsorship ensures you're on the radar of key decision-makers. Both are essential for progressing from an individual contributor to higher management and executive roles. They can also be the same person, and you should have more than one.

Example: Imagine you're working towards a promotion to a managerial position. A mentor might help you sharpen your leadership approach and prepare for the added responsibilities. At the same time, a sponsor within the company might advocate for your promotion in strategic meetings, influencing decision-makers to recognize your potential.

How to Cultivate Relationships That Open Doors

Building authentic relationships with mentors and sponsors doesn't happen overnight. It requires intentional effort and strategic networking.

Building Mentorship Relationships:

- **Be Proactive:** Don't wait for a mentor to come to you. Identify leaders you admire and reach out. A simple message expressing your admiration for their work and your desire to learn from them can be the starting point of a powerful mentorship.
- **Seek Mutual Value:** Mentorship shouldn't be one-sided. Find ways to add value to your mentor's life, whether it's through offering assistance, sharing an interesting article, or giving them feedback on initiatives they're involved in.
- **Be Respectful of Their Time:** Understand that mentors are often busy, so be concise and specific about what you're looking for. Prepare questions in advance to make your interactions as valuable as possible.

Cultivating Sponsorship Relationships:

- **Showcase Your Work:** Ensure your contributions are visible by sharing your successes in a way that highlights your leadership qualities. Document your achievements and share them with your sponsors.
- **Align Your Goals with Their Interests:** Sponsors are more likely to advocate for you

when your career goals align with their departments or organization's objectives. Understand their priorities and find ways to demonstrate how your growth contributes to those objectives.

- **Build Trust Over Time:** Sponsorship relationships often develop from a foundation of trust. Demonstrate your reliability and dedication, making it clear that you're serious about your career growth.

Example: If you're working in a cross-functional team, use that as an opportunity to showcase your leadership. If you've impressed a senior leader or peer in one project, casually ask them for a brief chat to discuss potential growth opportunities.

Tips for Navigating Cross-Identity Mentorship Dynamics

Mentorship and sponsorship relationships often cross lines of race, gender, and other identities, requiring awareness, intentionality, and strategic communication. While these relationships can be highly beneficial, they may also involve unique challenges, including unconscious bias, differing perspectives, and gaps in lived experience. The key to success lies in finding common ground, fostering open communication, and aligning on shared goals.

Strategies for Success:

- **Acknowledge Differences and Find Common Ground:** Instead of focusing on how you're different, look for shared values, goals, and professional interests. Differences in identity or lived experiences don't have to be barriers—they can be learning opportunities that enrich the relationship.
    - *Example:* You have a white senior executive mentor. Rather than shying away from discussing how your career experiences differ, you connect on leadership strategies, problem-solving, or industry insights—while also educating them on the unique challenges you may face.
    - **Tip:** *Approach these relationships with curiosity and mutual respect, ensuring both parties feel valued and heard.*
- **Establish Open and Direct Communicate:** Successful cross-identity mentorship requires clear and honest dialogue about expectations,

needs, and boundaries. Be upfront about what you hope to gain from the relationship and ask for guidance in areas where your mentor's perspective can add value.

- ○ **Example:** If you are seeking sponsorship from a senior leader who doesn't share your background, you might say: *I'm looking for guidance on positioning myself for leadership roles and navigating the challenges that can come with being one of the few Black professionals in executive spaces. I'd love to hear your perspective and any insights you have."*
- ○ **Tip:** *Be direct but adaptable. If you sense hesitation or discomfort from your mentor or sponsor, guide the conversation toward shared professional development topics first.*

- **Balance Learning and Teaching:** While mentorship is an opportunity for you to gain insight and guidance, it can also serve as a moment of learning for your mentor or sponsor. If they are unaware of the additional barriers you may face, share your experience in a constructive way.

  - ○ **Example:** *If a sponsor assumes traditional leadership paths work the same for everyone, you might say:* "One challenge I've faced is not always being in the rooms where key decisions are made. I'd love your advice on how I can increase my visibility and ensure my

contributions are recognized at the leadership level."
- **Tip:** *Instead of focusing solely on the obstacles, steer the conversation toward solutions and strategies that your mentor or sponsor can help you implement.*

- **Address Unconscious Bias with Strategy, Not Frustration:** Bias—whether implicit or explicit—can shape mentorship and sponsorship dynamics. Rather than internalizing it or avoiding difficult conversations, equip yourself with strategic ways to advocate for yourself.
  - ***Example:*** If your mentor unintentionally overlooks structural barriers that impact your career, shift the conversation to data-driven insights.
  "I recently read a study on how Black professionals often receive less direct feedback than their peers, which can impact career growth. I'd love your honest assessment of my leadership strengths and areas for improvement."
  - **Tip:** *Redirect the conversation to objective performance metrics and actionable feedback rather than personal anecdotes about bias.*

Be Selective and Intentional About Cross-Identity Mentorship:

Not all mentorship or sponsorship relationships are equally beneficial. If a mentor is unwilling to understand your experiences or a sponsor is hesitant to advocate for you, it may not be a productive relationship.
- ***Example:*** If a senior leader provides generic advice but doesn't actively

champion you for opportunities, consider redirecting your energy toward mentors or sponsors who actively invest in your success.

- **Tip:** *Look for mentors and sponsors who are willing to go beyond advice and take action—whether by introducing you to key decision-makers, advocating for your promotions, or amplifying your contributions.*

Additional Example: If you are navigating a mentorship relationship with a senior leader from a different racial or gender background, it's beneficial to approach each conversation with both an open mind and an assertive understanding of your goals. This might mean discussing past challenges you've faced and being open about your career ambitions while showing a genuine interest in their perspective and experiences.

Conclusion

The ability to secure and leverage both mentorship and sponsorship can make all the difference in your career growth. Cross-identity mentorship and sponsorship can be transformative, but they require intentionality, strategic communication, and mutual respect. By focusing on shared goals, maintaining direct and open communication, addressing bias constructively, and ensuring reciprocity, you can cultivate meaningful relationships that propel your career forward.

Chapter 11: Leading While Black

Understanding the Unique Burdens and Privileges of Being a Black Leader

Being a Black leader in a predominantly white or less diverse corporate environment is a unique experience filled with both challenges and opportunities. On one hand, you carry the weight of visibility, bias, and the pressure to over-perform. On the other hand, your leadership presents a powerful opportunity to drive change, shape inclusive policies, and inspire future leaders.

In this chapter we will explore the nuances of Black leadership, offering strategies to navigate bias, set boundaries, and create lasting impact while protecting your peace.

Understanding the Unique Burdens and Privileges of Being a Black Leader

- **The Pressure to Represent Your Entire Race:** You are not just leading—you are often expected to be the voice for all Black professionals in your organization. Whether intentional or not, colleagues may look to you for guidance on diversity-related matters, even when it's outside your expertise. This expectation can lead to exhaustion, **frustration, and a feeling of isolation**.

- ○ **How to Overcome It:** Instead of trying to carry the entire burden, redirect the responsibility to the organization by advocating for structured DEI programs, mentorship initiatives, and company-wide education. You don't have to be the only one doing the work.

- **Microaggressions and Stereotyping:** As a Black leader, you are more likely to encounter coded language, assumptions about your competence, or being "othered" in leadership spaces. Comments like *"You're so articulate"* or being assumed to be in a **lower-ranking role** are subtle but damaging.

  - ○ **How to Overcome It:** Address these incidents strategically rather than emotionally. If someone consistently dismisses your expertise, assert yourself by saying:
    "I appreciate your perspective, but my experience in [specific area] has proven otherwise. Here's what the data shows..."
  - ○ If microaggressions become persistent or systemic, document them and use your influence to push for company-wide bias training.

- **The Weight of Visibility:** Being one of the few or one of one Black leaders in an organization often means that your actions are scrutinized more closely. This visibility can make you feel like you're constantly being watched or assessed, influencing how you lead and interact. The pressure to be perfect, avoid mistakes, and remain "likable" can be overwhelming.

- **How to Overcome It:** Instead of focusing on appeasing perceptions, focus on performance, influence, and strategic positioning. Build a network of allies and sponsors who can vouch for your work, ensuring that your impact speaks louder than scrutiny.

Unique Privileges

- **An Opportunity to Break Barriers:** Being a Black leader is an act of defiance against systemic barriers. Your presence in leadership challenges traditional power structures and paves the way for future Black professionals.
- **Influence and Perspective:** Your unique lived experiences can bring diverse perspectives to decision-making processes and help push organizations towards more inclusive and innovative practices.

Example: You are the only Black leader in the executive suite. Instead of staying silent on DEI matters, you leverage your position to advocate for diverse hiring pipelines, push for sponsorship programs, and ensure pay equity audits are part of leadership discussions.

Your presence alone is not enough—it's how you use your platform that defines your leadership.

Strategies for Addressing Bias in Your Team or Organization

Addressing bias effectively requires strategic thinking and courage. Here are some practical strategies to tackle bias and foster a more equitable work environment as a strategic leader.

1. Educate and Train:

Implement training programs that focus on understanding bias, cultural competency, and inclusive leadership. Ensure that these programs go beyond one-time events and become part of continuous learning for the entire team.

2. Create Safe Spaces for Dialogue:

Encourage open conversations where team members can express their experiences and concerns without fear of judgment. As a leader, set an example by being vulnerable and sharing your own experiences with bias when appropriate. Employee Resource Groups can be a great resource

3. Hold Others Accountable:

Make it clear that bias will not be tolerated and that everyone in the team is responsible for maintaining an inclusive environment. Create mechanisms for reporting and addressing bias incidents confidentially.

4. Foster Mentorship and Sponsorship:

Support and mentor employees from underrepresented backgrounds and encourage others to do the same. Having a network of allies can amplify voices and create a culture of support.

How to Balance Being a Role Model with Protecting Your Peace

The dual role of being a leader and a representative for your community can sometimes feel like an impossible balancing act. Prioritizing your mental and emotional well-being is essential to sustain long-term effectiveness and leadership credibility.

Setting Boundaries:

As a leader, it's important to know when to say no and protect your time and mental energy. Communicate your boundaries clearly and assertively, so others understand and respect them.

Example: You don't have to be the DEI spokesperson for every conversation. Politely redirect by saying: *"I'm happy to discuss this, but I encourage the team to also consult DEI specialists who are experts in these areas."*

Practicing Self-Care:

Regularly engage in self-care practices that recharge your mind and body. This could be anything from therapy and meditation to taking a day off to disconnect. Remember, you cannot lead effectively if you are burned out.

Example: You block off one afternoon a month as "personal time" to disconnect from leadership stressors and recharge.

Leveraging Your Support Network:

Connect with other Black leaders or allies who understand your experience and can provide guidance or a safe space to decompress. These connections can offer insight, solidarity, and practical advice for handling specific challenges.

Example: You join a professional Black leadership network where you exchange strategies on navigating corporate politics and advancing into executive roles.

Balancing Act Exercise: Create a weekly reflection sheet that includes prompts such as:

- "What are my boundaries, and did I uphold them this week?"
- "Did I take time for self-care?"
- "What challenges did I face as a leader, and how did I manage them?"

Tracking these reflections helps you stay grounded, intentional, and resilient in your leadership journey.

Conclusion

Leading while Black is a responsibility, a challenge, and an opportunity. You are navigating spaces not designed for your success—yet you are thriving, building influence, and reshaping the corporate landscape.

By strategically addressing bias, setting boundaries, and leveraging your leadership position, you amplify your impact while protecting your peace.

Your leadership is more than just professional success—it's about transformation, legacy, and paving the way for others.

Next, we'll explore how to create a lasting legacy as a Black leader and the steps to ensure your leadership influence resonates for years to come.

Chapter 12: Resilience Without Burnout

Setting Boundaries to Protect Your Time and Mental Health

One of the most critical aspects of sustaining resilience as a leader is learning to set boundaries that protect your mental and emotional well-being. This chapter will focus on the importance of recognizing your limits and implementing strategies to maintain them.

Defining Personal Boundaries

- **What Are Boundaries?** Boundaries are the non-negotiable limits you set with yourself and others to maintain your mental and emotional health. They can be physical, emotional, or even digital.
- **Types of Boundaries:** Learn the different types of boundaries such as work-life boundaries, boundaries with colleagues, and boundaries around personal time.
- **Communicating Boundaries:** Clear, assertive communication is key. Practice using phrases like "I'm unavailable during this time," or "I need to step away to recharge."

Strategies for Effective Boundary Setting
- **Time Blocking:** Schedule blocks of time that are protected for self-care, strategic thinking, and personal activities. Treat these time blocks with the same priority as meetings or deadlines.
- **Digital Detox:** Set boundaries for your availability outside of work hours, such as no work emails or messages after 7 PM. This helps create mental space for personal life.
- **Saying No Without Guilt:** Learn to say no in a way that protects your energy. Practice phrases like "I'd love to, but I need to focus on my current priorities."

Recognizing and Addressing Burnout Before It Derails Your Progress

Burnout can strike at any time and can be especially dangerous for leaders who feel the pressure of maintaining high standards. This section will focus on recognizing the early signs of burnout and practical approaches to mitigate it.

Signs of Burnout

- **Physical Symptoms:** Chronic fatigue, headaches, muscle tension, and sleep disturbances.
- **Emotional Symptoms:** Feelings of overwhelm, irritability, checking out and reduced motivation.
- **Cognitive Symptoms:** Difficulty concentrating, forgetfulness, and indecisiveness.
- **Behavioral Changes:** Withdrawal from social interactions, procrastination, and a decline in performance.

Addressing Burnout Proactively

- **Schedule Regular Breaks:** Regular, scheduled breaks throughout the day can help prevent burnout. Use techniques like the Pomodoro method to keep your mind refreshed.
- **Mindfulness and Meditation:** Incorporate mindfulness exercises or meditation into your daily routine to help you stay grounded and reduce stress.
- **Delegate and Prioritize:** Learn to delegate tasks effectively and prioritize what truly matters. Accept that you can't do everything, and that prioritizing is a strength, not a weakness.

The Role of Therapy, Self-Care, and Community in Long-Term Success

Self-care and support systems are not just luxuries, they are essential components for long-term leadership success. This section will explore how therapy, self-care, and community play a vital role in maintaining resilience.

Therapy as a Leadership Tool

- **Reducing Stigma Around Mental Health:** Understand that seeking therapy is not a sign of weakness but a proactive way to manage stress and personal growth.
- **Developing Coping Strategies:** Therapy can help leaders develop healthy coping mechanisms for managing stress and navigating complex workplace dynamics.
- **Finding the Right Fit:** Tips on finding a therapist who understands your cultural and personal experiences and can provide tailored guidance.

Self-Care Practices for Sustainable Leadership

- **Physical Self-Care:** Regular exercise, adequate sleep, and a balanced diet are foundational to maintaining physical and mental energy.
- **Emotional Self-Care:** Activities that bring joy, relaxation, and emotional balance, such as hobbies, journaling, or time spent in nature.
- **Digital Self-Care:** Unplugging from screens, especially social media and work notifications, to rest your mind and build mental resilience.

The Power of Community

- **Building Your Network of Support:** Surround yourself with people who uplift you, challenge you, and support your growth. This can include peers, mentors, or community groups.

- **Leveraging Peer Support Groups:** Join or form peer-led support groups where leaders can share challenges, celebrate successes, and gain advice in a safe and confidential environment.
- **Connecting with Mentors and Allies:** Having people who understand your experiences and can advocate for you or give guidance is invaluable for long-term growth.

Reflection Exercise: "How does my self-care routine support my leadership? What adjustments can I make to ensure it's serving me effectively?"

Conclusion

Leading while Black is a complex balancing act—one that demands resilience, strategy, and an unwavering commitment to both personal and collective success. The challenges are undeniable: the pressure to represent, the scrutiny, the biases that persist even at the highest levels. Yet so are the opportunities—to break barriers, amplify change, and redefine what leadership looks like.

True leadership isn't just about navigating corporate spaces successfully; it's about reshaping them. By setting boundaries, advocating for equity, and mentoring the next generation, you ensure that your success isn't an anomaly but a blueprint for others to follow.

As you move forward in your leadership journey, remember:

✓ **You are not alone**. There is a community of Black professionals who understand your journey and can provide support.

✓ **Your voice carries power**. Use it to challenge bias, demand accountability, and create pathways for others.

✓ **Your well-being matters**. Success is not just about achievement—it's about sustainability and peace of mind.

Next, we'll explore how to pay it forward—how your leadership can leave a lasting impact by mentoring, sponsoring, and actively shaping the next generation of Black leaders.

Chapter 13: Pay It Forward

Becoming a Mentor/Sponsor and Advocate for Others

As leaders, one of the most powerful ways to impact future generations is to invest in the success of others. This section will focus on how to step into mentorship, sponsorship, and advocacy roles that empower others to thrive and advance in their careers.

Remember Mentorship vs Sponsorship

- **What is Mentorship?** A mentor is someone who provides guidance, support, and advice, helping others navigate their professional paths. They share their experiences, provide insights, and serve as a sounding board for challenges.
- **What is Sponsorship?** A sponsor is a leader who actively champions someone's career, using their influence to advocate for the individual's growth and advancement. This might involve recommending them for promotions, high-visibility projects, or networking opportunities.
- **Why Both Are Essential:** While mentorship can be more informal and advice-oriented, sponsorship requires a deeper level of active advocacy. Both play critical roles in empowering individuals to reach their potential.

Steps to Becoming an Effective Mentor/Sponsor

- **Identify Potential Mentees:** Look for individuals who show promise and are eager to grow. They might be team members, colleagues, or individuals within your professional network.

- **Listen and Build Trust:** Begin by creating an environment where your mentees feel safe to share their experiences, challenges, and ambitions. Building trust is crucial for an impactful mentorship or sponsorship relationship.

- **Provide Constructive Feedback and Guidance:** Share your experiences and lessons learned. Provide actionable feedback that can help mentees refine their approach and achieve their goals.

- **Advocate for Their Success:** Go beyond offering advice—actively advocate for their growth by highlighting their contributions, recommending them for key projects, and supporting their visibility in meetings and professional spaces.

Example: As a manager, you noticed a talented team member who had potential but lacked opportunities to showcase their skills. You decide to sponsor them, recommending them for a major project that leads to a promotion and more visibility within the organization. This act of sponsorship not only propelled the individual forward but also strengthened your reputation as a leader who nurtures talent.

Building a Legacy of Leadership That Reflects Your Values

True leadership is not just about personal success; it's about creating a lasting impact that aligns with your values and uplifts those around you. This section will focus on building a legacy that embodies your commitment to equity, inclusion, and empowerment.

Defining Your Leadership Values

- **What Are Core Leadership Values?** Identify what matters most to you as a leader. These could be integrity, empathy, advocacy, inclusivity, or resilience.
- **Aligning Actions with Values:** Ensure your actions consistently reflect these values, from decision-making to everyday interactions.
- **Passing Values on to Others:** Model your core values in a way that inspires those around you. Encourage your team members to adopt these values in their own work and interactions.

Creating a Lasting Impact

- **Recognition and Celebration:** Celebrate the achievements of those you mentor and sponsor, reinforcing a culture of appreciation and shared success.
- **Passing the Torch:** Ensure that your legacy is carried forward by preparing the next generation of leaders. Create systems for knowledge transfer and succession planning within your organization or community.
- **Empowering Others to Lead:** Encourage those you mentor and sponsor to take on leadership roles themselves and pay it forward, creating a cycle of growth and empowerment.

Contributing to Systemic Change from Within

Change doesn't happen overnight, and often it requires more than individual efforts. This section will focus on how leaders can contribute to systemic change within their organizations and industries to create environments where everyone can succeed.

Recognizing the Barriers

- **Understanding Systemic Challenges:** Analyze the specific barriers that exist in your organization or industry that prevent Black professionals and other marginalized groups from advancing.
- **Identifying Opportunities for Change:** Look for opportunities where systemic change can make a real impact, whether it's through policy changes, new programs, restructuring mentorship and sponsorship initiatives.

Strategies for Driving Change

- **Building Coalitions:** Collaborate with allies and other like-minded leaders to push for meaningful change. This can involve creating or joining task forces, ERGs, or coalitions within your company.
- **Advocating for Policy Change:** Use your voice to advocate for policies that promote inclusivity and equitable opportunities, such as fair promotion processes, unbiased performance reviews, or leadership training programs.
- **Championing Accountability:** Hold leadership accountable for supporting diversity, equity, and inclusion initiatives. Use data and

stories to demonstrate the importance of these initiatives and their impact.

Reflection Prompt: "What systemic changes do I believe are necessary in my workplace or industry? What role can I play in making these changes a reality?"

Conclusion

The journey of leadership is not just about personal growth but about lifting others up, creating a supportive network, and contributing to broader change. By paying it forward, you build a leadership legacy that aligns with your values, uplifts those around you, and leaves a meaningful impact on your industry.

Now you are ready to wrap all of this up and be on your way to your next level.

Conclusion: A Call to Lead

You've reached the end of this book, but your leadership journey is just beginning. The lessons, strategies, and exercises within these pages are meant to be more than just words—they are tools to help you step fully into your power, navigate challenges with confidence, and create lasting impact.

This book was designed to help you see that you have the power to cultivate the career that you desire on your own terms. While I may not have been able to cover every scenario and everything that you may have to think about and come up against, I did cover the most important key and that is you and who you are. If you get nothing else from this entire book, I want you to know that your authenticity is your greatest leadership asset.

Why Authenticity Matters in an Ecosystem that doesn't always see you

In spaces where fitting in is often rewarded more than standing out, choosing to lead in a way that reflects your true self is both revolutionary and necessary.

- **Building Trust and Respect:** Leaders who show up as their authentic selves naturally build trust. People want to follow leaders who are genuine and unapologetic about who they are.

This builds loyalty and fosters a culture where others feel safe to express their true selves too.

- **Fostering Innovation and Diversity:** When leaders prioritize authenticity, they open the door for diverse perspectives to flourish. Innovation thrives in environments where people can be themselves without fear of being sidelined or silenced.
- **Enduring Impact:** Leaders who remain true to themselves often leave a lasting legacy. Their actions and decisions inspire others not just to achieve but to aspire to lead in ways that align with their values and beliefs.

The truth is, corporate spaces may not have been designed with you in mind, but they need you—your perspective, your expertise, and your ability to drive meaningful transformation.

Action Plan: Taking the Next Steps in Your Leadership Journey

Now that you are ready to cultivate the career of your dreams here are the steps to lay out that path.

1. **Define Your Leadership Vision**
    a. Revisit the exercises from each chapter and refine your long-term leadership goals.
    b. identify what success looks like for you in the next year, five years, and beyond.
    c. Align your career moves with your values and impact-driven leadership approach.
2. **Strengthen Your Influence and Visibility**
    a. Advocate for yourself and others in leadership conversations.
    b. Develop a personal brand that reflects your expertise and leadership style.
    c. Seek speaking engagements, board opportunities, or industry leadership roles.
3. **Build a Strong Support Network**
    a. Identify mentors and sponsors who will champion your growth.
    b. Connect with Black leadership networks, affinity groups, and executive communities.
    c. Pay it forward by mentoring and sponsoring the next generation of Black professionals.

4. **Navigate Leadership Challenges with Confidence**
    a. Be proactive about addressing bias and holding your organization accountable.
    b. Set firm boundaries to protect your peace and longevity in leadership.
    c. Invest in self-care, therapy, or executive coaching to sustain your growth.
5. **Commit to Paying It Forward**
    a. Leadership isn't just about advancing your own career, it's about making the path easier for those who come after you.
    b. Identify one emerging Black professional you can mentor or sponsor.
    c. Use your influence to advocate for structural change in hiring, promotions, and leadership pipelines.
    d. Leave a legacy of inclusion and excellence that will outlast your tenure.

Final Thoughts

This journey has its obstacles, but you are not alone.

You Belong.

This is more than a slogan—it is a truth that must be fully embraced. Too often, many Black professionals question their place in spaces not originally designed for us. But the reality is this: your presence is necessary, your perspective is valuable, and your leadership is transformative. Every time you bring your authentic self to the table; you challenge the status quo and redefine what leadership looks like.

Your Leadership Matters.

Your journey—defined by resilience, excellence, and impact—has the power to reshape industries, uplift communities, and carve out opportunities for others. Leadership is more than a title, it's a responsibility. And in that responsibility lies the ability to ignite change, demand equity, and create a future where all Black professionals don't just navigate corporate spaces but thrive within them.

Now go forward, and let the world see the incredible leader you are—and the even greater leader you're becoming.

Connect with Me

For continued learning and professional development, connect with me through the following platforms:

Our Learning Platform:
https://visionarydevelopmentconsulting.learnworlds.com/

LinkedIn:
https://www.linkedin.com/in/sharittamarshallmba/

YouTube:
https://www.youtube.com/@VisionaryDevelopment

Let's continue the journey of growth, leadership, and success together.

About the Author

Sharitta Marshall, a Detroit native, an alum of Howard University, Arizona State University and a recovered survivor of corporate PTSD has transformed her personal experiences into a mission to support underrepresented and marginalized professionals—particularly Black employees. As a former Global ERG Leader and DEI Strategist, she witnessed how workplace barriers, from microaggressions to being undervalued, hinder career growth and professional fulfillment.

Drawing from her MBA, DEI and Instructional Design certifications, and extensive experience in SaaS, Ed Tech, and leadership, Sharitta designs professional development training programs that empower employees to navigate corporate spaces, advocate for themselves, and achieve leadership success.

She partners with ERGs and DEI leaders to create high-impact training solutions that drive career advancement, leadership development, and organizational change. She has worked with brands such as Chezie, Las Vegas Raiders, and SEEDSpot and is a sought-after speaker for industry events.

Sharitta is committed to equipping Black professionals and other marginalized employees with the tools to thrive, grow, and lead—without compromise.

www.ingramcontent.com/pod-product-compliance
Lightning Source LLC
Chambersburg PA
CBHW052141070526
44585CB00017B/1930